The All New Compendium of
Cardmaking
Techniques

D0257214

First published in Great Britain 2006

Search Press Limited
Wellwood, North Farm Road,
Tunbridge Wells, Kent TN2 3DR

Reprinted 2006 (twice), 2007

Based on the following books from the *Handmade Greetings Cards* series published by Search Press:

Card & Thread Greetings Cards by Polly Pinder (2004)
Watercolour Greetings Cards by Jane Greenwood (2004)
Quilled Greetings Cards by Diane Crane (2005)
Eyelet Greetings Cards by Polly Pinder (2005)
Quick Parchment Greetings Cards by Janet Wilson (2005)
Silk Ribbon Greetings Cards by Ann Cox (2005)
Beaded Greetings Cards by Patricia Wing (2005)
Three-Dimensional Greetings Cards by Dawn Allen (2005)
Glitter Greetings Cards by Polly Pinder (2005)

Text copyright © Polly Pinder, Jane Greenwood,
Diane Crane, Janet Wilson, Ann Cox, Patricia Wing
and Dawn Allen

Photographs by Roddy Paine Photographic Studios

Photographs and design copyright © Search Press Ltd. 2006

All rights reserved. No part of this book, text, photographs
or illustrations may be reproduced or transmitted in any
form or by any means by print, photoprint, microfilm,
microfiche, photocopier, internet or in any way known or as
yet unknown, or stored in a retrieval system, without
written permission obtained beforehand from Search Press.

ISBN 10 - 1 84448 161 1
ISBN 13 - 978 1 84448 161 3

The Publishers and author can accept no responsibility for
any consequences arising from the information, advice or
instructions given in this publication.

Suppliers
If you have difficulty in obtaining any of the materials and
equipment mentioned in this book, then please visit the
Search Press website for details of suppliers:
www.searchpress.com

Alternatively, you can write to the Publishers at the address
above, for a current list of stockists, including firms who
operate a mail-order service.

The All New Compendium of
Cardmaking
Techniques

SEARCH PRESS

Contents

Card & Thread Cards

by Polly Pinder

One of the lovely aspects of card and thread is that the structure of each threaded shape can look extremely complex, as if it must have taken hours of painstaking work to create, but once the simple technique has been mastered, stunning threaded shapes can be quickly and easily produced.

Some readers may remember a craft called 'pin and thread', in which rows of shiny-headed nails were banged into pieces of wood, then threads of string, wool, cotton, raffia or fine wire were wound round the nails to produce spectacular images. Card and thread is very similar. The principle is the same: the act of winding thread to create an image, but nails and pins are not required. Instead, notches, Vs or slits are cut into the card shape, then thread is wound round the shape and is caught and secured in the notches. A pattern is created, with the design governed by how many notches, Vs or slits are missed during the winding process. It sounds much more complicated than it is: once you get winding there'll be no stopping you, and the design possibilities are endless.

There are many beautiful papers and cards available to complement your card and thread designs: they come in all textures and shades and can be chosen from craft shops or picked up wherever you see them: I have used an office folder and a chocolate box lid whilst preparing cards for this book.

Striking new metallic threads are now available in a variety of plies and textures, and there are silky and satin threads in a multitude of colours, or multicoloured ones that vary in tone, all just waiting to be wound intriguingly into the shape of a flower, a cat or butterfly.

I have always believed that a beautifully handmade greetings card, created with patience and love, is equal to any expensive gift. It will always be treasured by the recipient. I hope that the step-by-step projects and the other cards shown in this section will generate enthusiasm and inspire readers to create many wonderful card and thread images.

Polly

Materials

Card and papers

The card used to make your greetings cards needs only to be stiff enough to stand up when folded in half and decorated with your card and thread artwork. The card used to make the shapes needs to be as rigid as possible so that pulling the threads across will not distort it. If your chosen card is not sturdy enough, it can always be backed by a piece of mount board.

There is a wonderful variety of cards and papers available today: from textured handmade papers to glossy or pearlescent card or self-adhesive foil – so be adventurous. Even old-fashioned wood chip wallpaper can look surprisingly effective. Highly textured papers made from cotton pulp make fascinating backgrounds: see the initialled heart on page 17. You can also decorate your own paper backgrounds: designs such as stripes can be produced on a computer, but lines carefully drawn with felt-tipped pen would be equally effective.

Stiff card for making shapes, shown with a variety of decorative cards and papers ideal for cardmaking.

Threads and embellishments

Exciting new metallic threads are now being manufactured. They come in a variety of plies and can be smooth and shiny or textured and sparkly. There are multicoloured silky threads; satin threads that have subtle changes of tone; brilliant greens, bright purples, iridescent blues and fluorescent oranges. I have used traditional and modern embroidery threads, wool and fine string for the designs in this book, but ordinary sewing cottons could also be used, as could anything which is fine enough to be caught in the little slits, Vs or notches of the card shapes.

Anything glittery, shiny or with an interesting texture can be used to embellish: beads, bindis and buttons; pipe cleaners; feathers and flat-backed gemstones. Craft stickers come in all shapes, sizes and colours and are available in most good craft shops. Rubber stamps and inkpads are excellent for decorating your cards and can also be bought from craft shops.

Threads and wool with embellishments: feathers, beads, tiny seed beads and a beading needle, craft stickers, pipe cleaners and flat-backed gemstones.

Other items

Cutting implements and accessories You will need a pair of sharp, pointed scissors and a good craft knife with extra blades. I prefer to use a knife with a strong, steel handle. You will also need a self-healing cutting mat and steel ruler. Craft punches and fancy-edged scissors are very useful. You will need a slightly smaller version of the traditional pinking shears to cut out some of the shapes in this book.

Glues and sticky tapes You need a tube of clear, all-purpose glue, a glue stick, sticky tape, double-sided tape and 3D foam squares.

Tracing paper, pencils and eraser You will need tracing paper to trace the templates and an HB pencil, an eraser and a pencil sharpener. A white pencil is used for tracing on to dark paper and card.

Bobbin holder This is useful to prevent bobbins rolling away when you are winding. Push two very large nails through a piece of polystyrene packing.

A cutting mat, steel ruler, deckle-edged and fine, sharp scissors, craft punches, rubber stamp and inkpad, 3D foam squares, hole punch, glue stick and all-purpose glue, bobbin holder, craft knife, white and HB pencils, sharpener, double-sided tape and sticky tape.

Basic techniques

The technique of card and thread is to wind the thread round the back and front of a card shape, catching it in slits, Vs or notches to secure it. Variety is achieved through the colour, texture and thickness of the thread, the distance between the slits and the number of slits missed when threading.

Transferring designs on to card

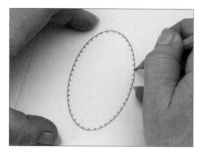  

1. Trace the design straight from the book or enlarge or reduce it on a photocopier to the size you require.

2. Turn the tracing paper over, place it on your card and go over the lines again with your pencil.

3. Cut carefully around the basic shape.

Cutting the card's edges

Threads are available in fine, medium and thick. The three cutting methods shown below can accommodate the varying degrees of thickness and texture in a thread. Metallic foil thread can be rather slippery and springy, so a slit in the card traps it more securely than a V or notch.

You can cut slits around the edge with a craft knife, on a cutting mat, or use very sharp, pointed scissors.

For thicker thread you will need V-shaped cuts, which can also be made with a craft knife or with sharp, pointed scissors such as nail scissors.

You can cut notches with deckle-edged craft scissors. You will need to practise to ensure that you end up with a balanced number of cuts ready for winding.

Winding

Winding involves securing the thread at the back of the shape, catching it in a notch, then taking the thread across the front of the card and missing a certain number of notches before catching it again. The thread is then wound round the back and up to the notch on the right of the starter notch.

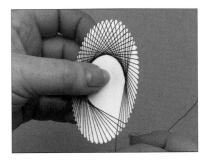

1. Secure the thread to the back of the card shape using a small piece of sticky tape. Take the thread to the edge, catch it in one of the notches and turn the shape over.

2. Miss however many notches are recommended in the project. Here I missed nineteen and caught the thread in the twentieth, then caught the second notch and the twenty-first, then the third and the twenty-second.

3. Continue wrapping the shape in this way until all the notches have been threaded.

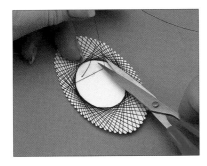

4. When the winding is complete, secure the thread at the back with another small piece of sticky tape and cut off the end.

Tip
Some metallic threads have a mind of their own and spring out of the V shape when the winding reaches a particular point. To avoid this, keep securing the thread at the back.

Winding is started by catching the thread in the first notch. These different effects are created by varying the number of notches that are missed before catching the thread again. The more notches that are missed, the smaller the central hole will be (see the shape on the left). If the thread is taken directly across a shape at its halfway point, as in the middle shape, there will be no hole. If only a few notches are missed, as in the right-hand shape, the hole will be quite large.

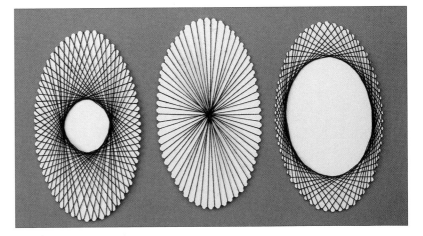

Heart of Gold

A handmade card book would not be complete without a project concerning matters of the heart. This card is quite dramatic: the thread is thicker than usual and the image is large in relation to the size of the card. The heart-shaped craft punch is produced to a standard size. If you cannot find this size, you will need to change the size of the embellished corners accordingly.

You will need

Cream card blank, 115mm (4½in) square

Red card, 100 x 150mm (4 x 6in)

Gold paper, 50 x 100mm (2 x 4in)

Thick gold thread

Heart craft punch, heart 12mm (½in) wide

Tracing paper and HB pencil

Craft knife and cutting mat

Sticky tape

Glue stick

3D foam squares

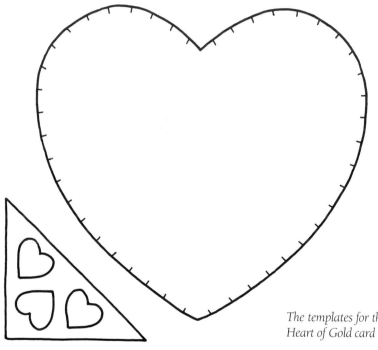

The templates for the Heart of Gold card

1. Trace the heart design, transfer it on to red card and cut it out. Use your craft knife and cutting mat to cut little Vs at each pencil mark round the edge.

Tip
The thread used here is quite thick. When you use thicker thread, make sure you cut the Vs larger than usual.

2. Secure the thread at the back of the heart with a piece of sticky tape and start winding at the second V to the right of the centre. This is your first V. Counting clockwise, leave eleven Vs empty, catch the twelfth, then go round the back to the second, on to the thirteenth and so on. Stop winding when you reach the second V left of the centre.

3. There will now be a central hole. In order to fill it, wind from the middle top of the heart, between the Vs on either side of the centre. Miss eleven Vs and catch the twelfth, then go back to the centre, then catch the thirteenth, and so on. Continue winding from the centre to fill the left-hand side of the hole in the same way. Secure at the back using sticky tape.

4. Transfer the corner shape on to red card twice and cut the two pieces out. Draw round these pieces on gold paper and cut out two gold corner pieces slightly smaller than the red ones.

5. Turn the heart craft punch upside down and punch out the little hearts from the red corners using the traced hearts as a positioning guide.

6. Carefully stick a gold paper corner to the back of each red corner.

7. Position the two corners diagonally opposite each other on the card blank and secure using a glue stick. Position and stick down the little punched out hearts in the two remaining corners.

8. Attach three 3D foam squares to the back of the threaded heart and secure it to the greetings card.

14

The thicker gold thread used here gives the card a wonderfully dramatic feel, with hot red, gold and the cool cream background combining to make a sumptuous gift for someone you love.

For these cards, a softer look is achieved by using pastel shades and non-metallic thread. For the long, pink card, the handmade tissue paper was stuck on using a glue stick. The tiny pearlescent hearts are often used to scatter on the tables at wedding feasts.

Opposite: For the little red card, the highly textured paper was stiff enough to make the actual greetings card. A piece of ordinary paper would need to be inserted to write the greeting.

The printing stamp for the heart-shaped card was made from a piece of polystyrene packing.

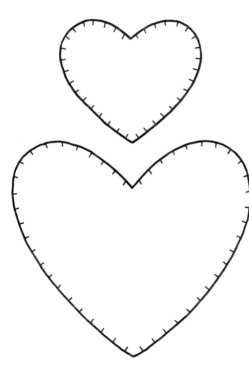

Templates for the threaded shapes on these cards

16

Bubbly Fish

These two goldfish, swimming in a sea of bubbles, can be threaded very easily once the shapes have been cut and the little slits round the edges have been made. Each fish has a body and a separate tail. The bubbles are threaded and caught in slits in the top and bottom edges of the card. These threads are not wound round, but secured at the top and bottom of the reverse side and neatly covered by a piece of card.

You will need
Pale blue card blank,
100 x 210mm (4 x 8½in)

Darker blue card, 100mm
(4in) square

Two strips of pale blue card,
15 x 95mm (⅝ x 3¾in)

Small piece of bronze
self-adhesive card

Fine embroidery thread in
various shades of orange

Pale blue embroidery thread

Ninety tiny gold beads and
beading needle

Single hole punch

Double-sided tape

Sticky tape

Clear all-purpose glue

Tracing paper, HB pencil,
white pencil and eraser

Craft knife and cutting mat

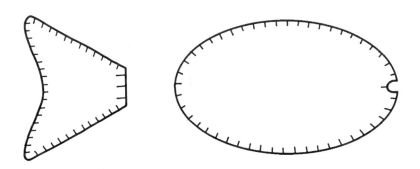

The templates for the Bubbly Fish card

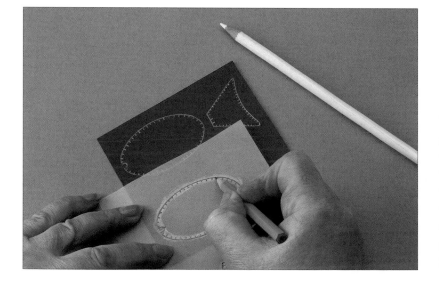

1. Trace the fish shapes. Turn the tracing paper over and scribble over the images with the white pencil. Lay the tracing right-side-up on the darker blue card and transfer the images by drawing over the lines with a sharp HB pencil. Repeat for the second fish.

2. Carefully cut out the card shapes and, using a craft knife and cutting mat, cut small slits at each pencil mark. Rub out any remaining white pencil using an eraser.

3. Secure the orange thread with sticky tape at the back of a fish body shape. Catch the thread through the slit in the mouth and take it to the twenty-fourth slit directly opposite. Take it back up behind, catch the second slit, then go over to the twenty-fifth and so on.

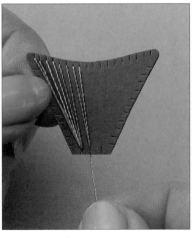

4. When the first round is complete, catch the slit fourth from the mouth, leave fifteen slits and catch the sixteenth. Go behind and up to the fifth, across to the seventeenth and so on. Secure at the back after the fourth slit on the other side of the mouth.

5. Secure the thread and hold the tail as shown. The tail has three slits at the narrow end. Start from the left-hand slit and wind to the six left-hand slits at the wider end, working left to right. Then wind from the middle slit to the six middle slits, and from the right-hand slit to the six right-hand slits.

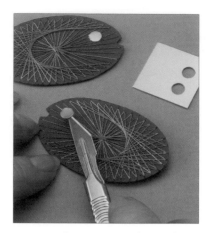

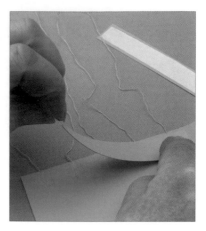

6. Next, holding the tail as shown, catch the first slit on one side and take the thread down to the last slit on the opposite side. Go behind and up to the second slit, then down to the penultimate slit on the opposite side. Continue until all the slits have been threaded, and secure at the back.

7. Punch two eyes from the bronze self-adhesive card and stick one on to each fish.

8. Separate the pale blue embroidery thread into five strands. Cut five small slits on the top and bottom edges of the front of the card blank, 12mm (½in) from each side, with 19mm (¾in) between them. Secure each strand with sticky tape close to the top of the other side. Stick double-sided tape to the card strips and use one to cover the ends of the strands.

9. Thread the needle, then thread eighteen beads on to each strand. Cross the three central strands over and secure these, and the two vertical strands, at the bottom of the reverse side. Cover the ends of the strands with the other strip of card.

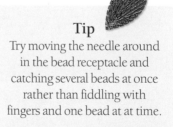

Tip
Try moving the needle around in the bead receptacle and catching several beads at once rather than fiddling with fingers and one bead at at time.

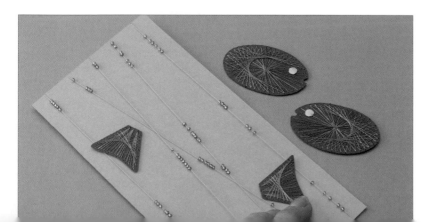

10. Slide the beads up and down the strands to make spaces for the fish. Using the all-purpose glue, stick each tail to the card first, then position and stick the bodies.

This bubbly underwater card adds a whole new dimension to the card and thread technique since threads are used to decorate the background card as well as the shapes.

Opposite: The gorgeous green underwater scene at top left features seaweed made from strips of green transparent film stuck on to the card with a glue stick. The little gold fish are craft stickers.

The bubbles on the pale blue card are bindis which were bought for the bridesmaids at my daughter's Indian wedding. Flat-backed gemstones are similar decorations available from most craft shops.

Above: I could not resist the lovely corrugated paper for this card. Finding metallic thread to match the blending colours of the paper was a bonus.

Watercolour Cards

by Jane Greenwood

In my thirty years as an illustrator I have always kept watercolour painting as a valued hobby. For my work I use inks for their permanence. The joy of watercolour, by contrast, is its spontaneity: rather than planning rigidly how you are going to paint a subject, you can let accidents and surprises happen – like the little fish in the aqueous painting at bottom left. Here, washes used with salt looked like a marine landscape, so I added fish to complete the picture. Surprises like this make ideal artwork for cards.

The chicken on the card featured in this section was made up, but I have included a simple outline which you can trace to give structure to your painting. You can trace a chicken picture from a book or magazine if you prefer.

Decorative items give a fun, three-dimensional effect to watercolour cards and all sorts of interesting bits can be found at craft shops, around the house or on walks.

I do hope this section will inspire card makers who have been discouraged by watercolours due to the impression that they are too difficult. Don't be put off! Following these simple steps, you will quickly get the knack and appreciate their ease and rapidity of use. I hope that the watercolourists who buy this book will also be inspired by the ideas shown. Good luck and I hope you enjoy yourselves as much as I did when making the cards for this section.

Jane A Greenwood.

Materials

Greetings cards are small in scale, and so I have used very simple materials sold in high street shops, such as paint sets, small pads of watercolour paper and a few brushes, sponges and things from the bathroom cupboard like cotton buds and paper tissues.

Paper

Watercolour paper comes not only in loose sheets but also in many different sized pads and blocks, and in different weights and textures. Some pads are sealed round the edges and some are spiral-bound. It is best to buy these in the heavier weights such as 250–300gsm (90–140lb) so that the paper will not buckle when wet. You do not need to buy anything larger than an A4 format for the paintings, and one sheet of 25 x 27.5cm (9 x 10¾in) watercolour paper for a background card.

Tracing paper also comes in pads, which are easier to use and keep clean and flat than large, unwieldy sheets. You can buy specially made card blanks and card in larger sheets to cut down in all colours from art and craft shops. Make sure you buy card that is stiff enough on which to mount the watercolour paintings.

Sketchpads are useful for planning the design of your card. You do not need to buy a professional one – a children's sketchpad is fine.

Card blanks, card, paper, self-adhesive memo notes, tracing paper, watercolour pads and blocks and a sketchpad.

Painting materials

The little watercolour paint sets I use were perfect for this book. They contain all the primary colours and the few secondary colours that you will ever need and they even come with a palette and brush!

I have used a few good quality watercolour paints in tubes for mixing up larger washes. The Artists' colours are more expensive but have more brilliance and transparency. I have used Prussian blue, viridian, cadmium yellow, cadmium red, burnt umber, yellow ochre, cerulean blue, alizarin crimson, cadmium lemon, lemon yellow and ultramarine blue for the cards shown in this section. White gouache is useful for spattering as it is opaque, and it can also be used for painting lines around paintings on coloured mounting card.

You'll need one large palette for mixing washes and a small selection of brushes. I tend to use a very large brush, a no. 12 round with a good point for most work; a couple of smaller rounds, numbers 6, 4 and 2 for the detail and a rigger, so called because it is used for painting the rigging on ships, for very fine detail. The flat brushes are useful for washes: I used a long broad one and a smaller one.

A toothbrush is used to spatter paint and kitchen salt to create lovely cracked effects in a wet wash. A candle can be used to create wax resist, cotton buds for mopping up little mistakes and paper tissues for bigger spillages! A natural sponge can be used to apply or lift off paint. I always use a sawn-off plastic water bottle for my water as the base is sturdy and broad.

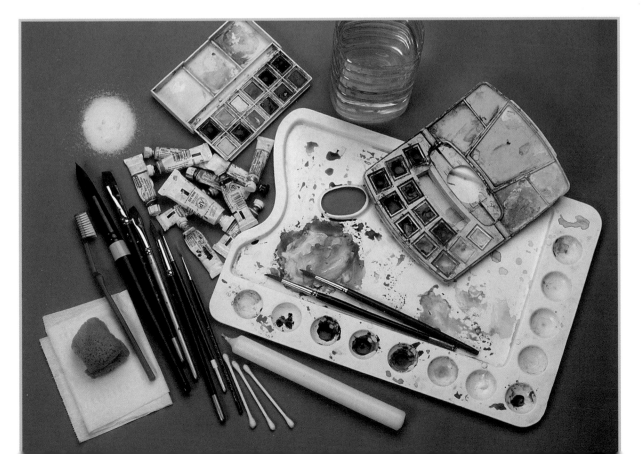

Watercolour tubes and paint sets, white gouache, a water container, palette, brushes, candle, cotton buds, toothbrush, sponge, paper tissue and kitchen salt.

Other materials

I used a handful of disposable push-up pencils for a nice fine line, a fatter, soft-leaded push-up pencil for sketching and tracing, and those lovely metallic gold gel pens for drawing a border round a card or for writing inside a dark-coloured card.

I always use a good cutting mat to cut the card as it has nice straight lines as guides and is kind to the knife blades. I usually use a heavy-duty craft knife to cut the card and a smaller scalpel for scoring paper or cutting out holes to introduce embellishments in a card.

For mounting card I used very thin double-sided tape, a tube of all-purpose glue and a can of spray mount which can be used with thin, smooth paper. You can use 3D foam squares when you want a raised effect. You will need two different pairs of scissors for cutting the sticky tape and the feathers and a putty eraser to clean up smudges of pencil when working with tracings. The little set squares and rulers can be bought in any supermarket; they are intended for children but are perfect for these little jobs.

Masking fluid is essential for blocking out shapes that you want to stay white while you are painting a darker background.

A cutting mat, ruler, craft knives and blades, paper scissors, putty eraser, all-purpose glue, spray mount, 3D foam squares, double-sided tape, set squares, masking fluid, push-up pencils, gold gel pens and nail scissors.

28

Decorative items

With the enormous range of products now produced for card makers, one is tempted while wandering around a craft shop to think not 'What can I find for that particular project?' but, 'Oh what fun! What can I do with that?' In this way the embellishments provide the springboard to new card ideas.

  I have bags containing little strips of coloured card for choosing frames; packets of leaf skeletons and bags of pretty, dyed duck feathers in all colours. Most of my feathers have been collected on visits to country houses with peacocks. The dusky coloured lady peacock feathers are very beautiful, as are guinea fowl and pheasant feathers. Ordinary things found around the house can also be used, such as cotton wool balls for bunny tails and string for a cow's tail.

Cotton wool balls, dyed duck feathers, natural feathers and household string.

Basic techniques

A graduated wash

This is the first thing you learn when getting accustomed to watercolours. A wash is used mostly for backgrounds but can be the subject of a painting, too. In this case we are making a graduated wash to look like a sky.

1. Mix Prussian blue with three times as much water. Take the no. 12 brush and brush across the paper in horizontal strokes from the top downwards, adding more water as you reach the bottom. Never go back over the wet paint.

2. Tip the paper to accentuate any effects you desire as the paint spreads into the water.

You will need

Small watercolour pad, 300gsm (140lb)

Brushes: no. 12 and no. 6 round, flat

Watercolours: Prussian blue, viridian, cadmium yellow

White gouache

Toothbrush

Salt

Natural sponge

Masking fluid

White candle

Spattering

The basic wash looked like a seascape to me, so I added some rocks and sea spray to create a feeling of movement. You can spatter using a paintbrush or a toothbrush.

Tip
Practise both techniques first so that you can control the direction of the spatters.

Load the brush with white gouache and flick the brush diagonally across the paper. Keep the brush at least 7.5cm (3in) from the paper.

A toothbrush can be used if you want the spatters to spread freely over a large area.

Wet in wet

This technique involves dropping colours into a wet wash. Surprising effects can occur when colours are mixed in this way and one spreads slowly into the other.

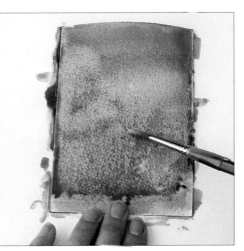

1. Using the larger brush, paint a wash of Prussian blue. Then load the brush with viridian and drop the green into the blue. Watch the colours spread and mix.

2. Take the smaller brush and drop a mix of cadmium yellow in to the lighter areas of green. Clear water can also be dropped in to lighten the washes.

Using salt

While washes are very wet, you can experiment with salt crystals which create unusual patterned effects.

1. While the washes are wet, sprinkle salt on the paper and watch the effects begin as the paint dries.

2. When dry, the salt can be removed using a dry brush.

3. I decided that the salt effects produced during this demonstration looked like a marine landscape, so I lifted out a couple of fish shapes with a clean, dry brush.

Lifting out

Once you have created a graduated wash, you can invent a landscape by lifting out paint to create a cloudy sky or simply by lightening the horizon to suggest the sea. You could also add a field or a beach in this way.

1. Using a small sponge, soaked in water and squeezed out, lift out cloud shapes from the wet wash. Roll the sponge over so that you are using a paint-free area each time.

2. Take a small, flat brush and drag it through the still wet wash two-thirds of the way down the painting, to suggest a horizon.

Masking

You can paint a simple image with masking fluid, either on white paper or on top of a light wash. Then paint a wash over it. When the wash is dry, the masking fluid can be rubbed off with your finger and a startling white image or an area of lighter wash is saved. This can be left as it is, painted in another colour or given form using shadow and tone.

1. Paint a simple shape using masking fluid and an old brush. Wash out the brush immediately.

2. When the masking fluid is dry, wash over the top with Prussian blue. Thin the wash at the bottom of the painting.

3. When the wash is dry, rub off the masking fluid with a clean finger.

Wax resist

A candle or a piece of candle can create a resist over which to paint in watercolour. This is quicker but less precise than using masking fluid.

Tip
Direct a strong light on to the paper while using the candle so that you can see what you are drawing.

1. Use a white wax candle to draw a simple design.

2. Apply your wash over the candle wax and the design will appear.

You can cut out the paintings with fancy-edged scissors or paint a wavy frame around them. Mount them on card in a contrasting colour or tone.

Chicken on the Run

I have a bird table in the garden and I had a loved budgie in a cage who lived to be eleven years old, a record I think! Birds are fascinating and one appealing image is of the brainless chicken dashing around, feathers flying, ridiculous and endlessly amusing. My large collection of feathers has been enlarged greatly by the feathers collected in friends' gardens: pretty, speckled bantam feathers, and long, green cockerel tail feathers.

You will need

Smooth satin watercolour paper, 12.5 x 18cm (5 x 7in) 300gsm (140lb)

Brushes: no. 6 round and rigger

Watercolours: cadmium yellow, cadmium red, yellow ochre and burnt umber

Tracing paper

Orange card, at least 380 x 140mm (15 x 5½in)

Large soft pencil, fine, hard pencil and putty eraser

Craft knife and cutting mat

Ruler or set square

Feathers

Toothbrush

Double-sided tape

All-purpose glue

1. Work over scrap paper. Trace the chicken using a soft pencil. Turn the tracing over and use the same pencil and a craft knife to scrape graphite over the traced lines.

2. Rub the graphite gently along the lines of the drawing with your finger.

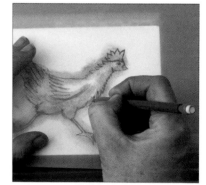

3. Turn the tracing over again and place it on your watercolour paper. Draw over the image with a fine, hard pencil to transfer it on to the paper.

4. Redraw the image using a fine pencil and removing any smudges with a putty eraser.

5. Take a no. 6 brush and a mix of cadmium yellow and yellow ochre, and paint around the pencil marks to outline the chicken image.

6. Wash in the middle of the chicken using a thin wash of cadmium yellow.

7. Paint the shadow of the chicken's wing using the darker mix. Use a clean, moist brush to lift out highlights from the wing, giving the chicken form.

8. Use cadmium red to paint the legs, feet, crest and beak.

9. Use burnt umber to pick out the shadows on the chicken's crest, the eye and the outline of the beak.

10. Use a rigger brush and some burnt umber added to the yellowy colour to accentuate the chicken's feathery outline. Add dark brown tones to the legs and feet using burnt umber.

11. Use yellow ochre and cadmium yellow to wash pale streaks on to the ground. Add brown streaks mixed from burnt umber and yellow ochre for a straw-like texture. Allow to dry.

12. Dip a toothbrush in cadmium yellow, cadmium red and yellow ochre, without mixing the paints well. Pull back the bristles with your finger and spatter the paint over the chicken.

13. Use a craft knife to cut along the edge of the feathers on the chicken's wing.

14. Push feathers into the holes in the paper, and arrange them to look like the chicken's tail.

15. Apply double-sided tape to the back of the card to secure the feathers in place.

16. Trim the chicken painting so that the tail feathers overlap the top. Place it on orange card folded at the side, judging the width of the borders by eye. Using a craft knife and cutting mat, cut out the orange card. The front of my card measures 190 x 140mm (7½ x 5½in). Remove the backing from the double-sided tape. Apply all-purpose glue to back of the chicken painting and stick it to the card.

17. Draw a line around the orange card a little way from the chicken painting, using a pencil and a straight edge.

18. Paint over the pencil line using a rigger brush and burnt umber mixed with cadmium red.

This handsome chicken looks as though he is in a tearing hurry. The humour of the painting is in the movement caused by the brush strokes on the ground, the spatters and the chicken's racing legs.

The addition of the feathers gives some of these birds a comical look, and you can choose outrageous colours to complete the effect. The robin and goose pictures would make ideal Christmas cards. The goose shows how you can make a really effective card using only one colour and a simple image.

Quilled Cards

by Diane Crane

For as long as I can remember I have been fascinated by paper of all kinds. One of my earliest memories is of sitting on the floor at home surrounded by bits of paper and being completely absorbed as I worked away with scissors and glue for hours on end. Well, not much has changed, except that I now favour sitting at the dining room table!

Over twenty years ago, a friend introduced me to the craft of paper quilling. I was instantly drawn to this unusual way of working with paper. Shortly afterwards, I discovered the existence of the Quilling Guild, which fired my enthusiasm still further. Having tackled many of the quilling patterns available at the time, I began to take my first tentative steps in designing my own patterns, and as I experimented with different techniques, I realised that the possibilities were endless, limited only by the imagination of the quiller.

After a few years of quilling for my own pleasure, I was given the opportunity to share my discoveries with others through teaching a weekly class. Cardmaking using quilled motifs has proved to be the most popular application of the craft. I frequently hear stories from quillers who have sent cards that were treasured, and sometimes even framed, by the recipients.

Quilling may not be the speediest of crafts, but it is certainly one of the most rewarding. Narrow strips of coloured paper are brought to life by the simple act of rolling, and a colourful world of paper coils and spirals opens up before your eyes. Everything you need is readily available: paper, scissors, glue and a willing set of fingers... so you can quill away to your heart's content!

Diane Crane

There are endless possibilities with paper. Here are a selection of cards illustrating the different effects you can achieve by using the quilling techniques demonstrated on the following pages.

Materials

Paper strips

These are pre-cut in a number of different widths and come in a wide variety of colours, from delicate pastels through to vibrant shades in every colour of the rainbow. A standard quilling strip in Britain is 450mm (17¾in) in length, and the strips are usually packed in a figure of eight arrangement. I like to open out the papers and store them in shallow cardboard trays, as the strips are easier to work with if they are flat. The most common width of paper is 3mm (⅛in) which is suitable for beginners. Fringed flowers are usually made from 5mm (³⁄₁₆in) wide paper, although you can use 3mm (⅛in) paper for smaller flowers. Strips which are 2mm (³⁄₃₂in) wide will give a still finer appearance to your quilling. You can use paper which is just 1mm (¹⁄₃₂in) wide particularly for making fine spirals. Occasionally much wider strips are used such as 10mm (³⁄₈in) and 15mm (⅝in).

Paper quilling strips. From the top: 10mm (³⁄₈in), 5mm (³⁄₁₆in), 3mm (¹⁄₈in) and 2mm (³⁄₃₂in) strips. Not shown as actual size.

Quilling essentials

Quilling tool

Various tools are available commercially. The best tool to use is one which has a fine slit, and the slit should be deep enough to accommodate the width of your paper strip. If the slit is too wide, the paper slips about and you will find it difficult to make a start. The paper should fit snugly in the slit so that it stays in position once you start to roll. An added advantage is that a fine tool will produce a coil which has a small centre. This will always make your quilling look more attractive.

Glue and fine-tip applicator

PVA is the best glue to use and a fine-tip applicator will produce a very fine line with a gentle squeeze of the bottle.

Cocktail sticks

Use to apply tiny amounts of glue and also to pick up and position individual pieces of quilling.

Scissors

It is well worth investing in a good quality pair of scissors. I use embroidery scissors which have extremely sharp, short blades for precision work and another pair for general cutting.

Florist wire

Collect lengths in different gauges. You can make spirals by winding a strip around wire and then removing it.

Ceramic tile

A ceramic tile is a useful smooth surface to make eccentric coils on. Alternatively, you could use a jam jar lid.

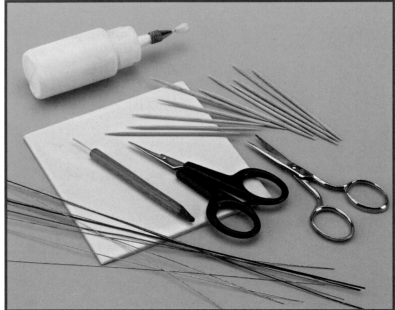

Other items

You will need a **ruler** when measuring and cutting your strips. You can make your own version from a piece of stiff card with the most common measurements marked on it, i.e: 75mm (3in), 150mm (6in).

Make a collection of **pearl-headed pins** with heads of different sizes. They are useful for moulding a solid coil into a dome.

A wide range of **blank cards** are available from good stationers and art shops. Aperture cards are useful, but you can cut your own shapes to fit a particular design with a little patience – and a steady hand! Mostly I buy flat sheets of card and cut my own. A **2H pencil** will give you an accurate line when measuring up a card and a **compass** is handy for drawing circular apertures.

When cutting with a **scalpel** take care because the blades are very sharp. Always cut against a **metal ruler** if you're making straight cuts. **Self-healing mats** are useful for cutting out apertures. The special surface prolongs the life of your blade and the 'wound' heals over as the name would suggest, so you can cut on it over and over again. They are sold in various sizes, but an A4 size is fine for most jobs.

Chalk pastels are wonderful for making subtle backgrounds for your quilling. They can turn a plain white card into something special. Pastels are available from art shops, and can be purchased individually or in boxed sets. You can use blunt scalpel blades for scraping small amounts of chalk pastel onto your card. Remember that pastels do not 'take' on card which has a smooth surface.

Tissue paper is available in a variety of colours. Squares of tissue paper can be wound diagonally around a piece of florist wire to make paper sticks. Tissue paper can also be used as a background for cards. For adding details such as facial features to your quilling, a **fine black pen** will be useful.

It is worth building up a collection of **paper and card offcuts**. You can use all kinds of bits and pieces when making quilled cards. Coloured envelopes from birthday cards are good for spiral roses and foil chocolate wrappers (with paper backing) are useful for spiralling. But beware – you soon might not be able to get into your house!

Storage is often a problem with quilling – there are so many tiny pieces to keep safe. I keep all kinds of small, shallow **boxes** to house my quilling.

Clockwise from bottom: blank aperture cards, different-coloured card, foil paper, different-coloured tissue paper, self-healing cutting mat, scalpel, 2H pencil, fine black pen, compass, handmade ruler, plastic ruler, metal ruler, pearl-headed pins, chalk pastels.

Tip
When not in use, store your fine-tip glue applicator upside down in a small container. This will help the glue to flow easily.

Basic techniques

Before you begin, take a close look at a quilling strip. One side is smooth with edges that turn down slightly and the other side is not. Take some time to feel the difference between your fingers. Always roll with the smooth side on the outside, as this will help to make your quilling more uniform.

When you are rolling a strip for the first time, resist the temptation to roll too tightly. People think that if they relax the tension, the coil will unravel but this is not the case. The rolled paper will only expand to its natural size. Quilling is a bit like knitting in the sense that the patterns may be the same but everyone's tension is different! Practise with 3mm (⅛in) strips before attempting to quill with finer strips of paper.

You will need

Eight 3mm (⅛in) paper strips, 150mm (6in) long

One 2mm (³⁄₃₂in) paper strip, 150mm (6in) long

One 3mm (⅛in) paper strip, 450mm (17¾in) long

Quilling tool

Scissors

Fine-tip glue applicator

Cocktail sticks

Metric ruler

Tissue paper square, 50 x 50mm (2 x 2in)

Paper square, 20 x 20mm (¾ x ¾in)

Tile or jam jar lid

A basic coil

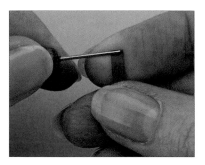

1. Line the strip up on the tool and start to turn.

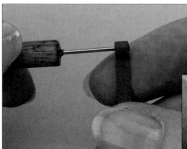

2. Turn the tool so that the strip winds tightly around it.

3. When the whole strip is wound on, release it and remove the coil.

4. Put a dot of glue at the end of the strip. The less glue you use, the better your quilling will be!

5. Poke a cocktail stick into the coil and press against it as you close the coil.

A finished basic coil

Shapes

Each of the shapes that follow started off as a basic, glued coil. Hold the coil between your fingers and thumbs in the general shape before you make a definite pinch.

*Use your thumbs and forefingers to squeeze a coil into a **teardrop** shape.*

*Use both thumbs to make an **eye** shape.*

*Make another eye and then shape it into a **square**.*

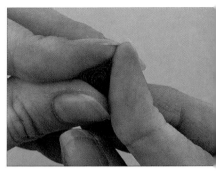

*Start with a teardrop and pinch it into a **triangle**.*

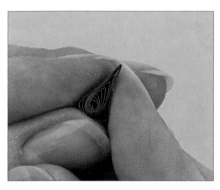

*Make another teardrop and shape it into a **long triangle**.*

Basic coil   *Teardrop*   *Eye*

Square   *Long triangle*   *Triangle*

Tip

When making shapes, always pinch your coil at the glued join. This disguises the join and avoids it appearing in an awkward place.

Peg

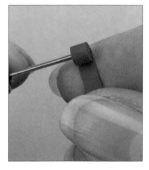

A finished peg

1. Roll a coil but do not let go when it is wound.

2. Glue the end of the strip down and then tap the peg down on the table.

3. Gently twist a cocktail stick in the hole to make the centre smooth.

Solid coil

1. Start off the coil by hand. Make it as tight as possible.

2. Now roll the coil by hand. Do not let go when it is wound.

3. Glue down the end. Your coil should be solid in the centre as shown.

A finished solid coil

Eccentric coil

1. Make a coil on the tool using an entire 450mm (17¾ in) strip, release it and glue down the end.

2. Now rewind the centre as shown and then let go.

3. Use a cocktail stick to gently even up the loops.

Tip
Making eccentric coils takes a little practice. Do not be discouraged if your first attempt is not as perfect as the one pictured. Keep trying!

4. Put a dab of glue on a tile or jam jar lid and place the coil on top.

A finished eccentric coil

Spirals

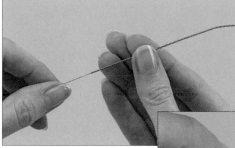

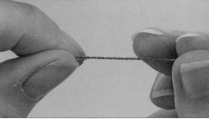

1. Cut a 2mm (^{3}/$_{32}$in) strip down the centre to create two 1mm (^{1}/$_{32}$in) strips. Dampen the end of a 1mm (^{1}/$_{32}$in) strip with saliva and carefully wind it on to a piece of wire at a 45° angle.

2. Wind the strip around the wire and then carefully remove the wire. Now gently stretch out the curled strip.

Spiral roses

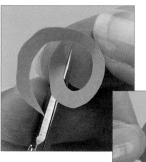

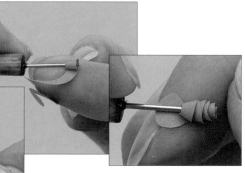

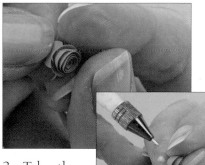

1. Cut off each corner of a paper square in a curve to make a circle. Then cut a spiral into the circle.

2. Roll it on to your tool.

3. Take the rose off the tool, release it slightly and glue the end down.

Paper sticks

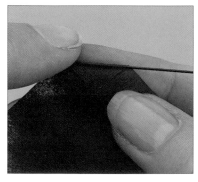

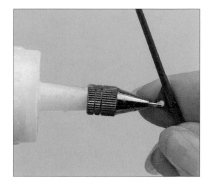

1. Fold the corner of a tissue paper square over a piece of wire and secure with glue.

2. Roll the tissue paper tightly around the wire.

3. Glue the end down and gently remove the wire.

Bloomin' Lovely

I like to experiment with all kinds of different subjects for designs but I always enjoy coming back to flowers. A simple flower in a pot is straightforward to put together and involves just a few of the basic shapes. I have chosen different shades of one colour but you can have some fun deciding on your own colour scheme. The following steps explain how to make one flower. Use the same technique to make four more flowers and complete the design.

You will need

For the flowers, 3mm (¹⁄₈in) strips:
40 strips in five shades of pink, 112mm (4½in) long, eight of each colour
10 green, 75mm (3in) long
5 green, 30mm (1³⁄₈in) long

For the flowerpots, 3mm (¹⁄₈in) strips:
15 brown, 112mm (4½in) long
5 brown, 45mm (1¾in) long

For the border, 2mm (³⁄₃₂in) strips:
2 brown, 450mm (17¾in) long

Quilling tool

Scissors

Fine-tip glue applicator

Cocktail sticks

Metric ruler and pencil

Blank card,
210 x 148mm (8¼ x 5¾in)

White paper,
160 x 45mm (6¼ x 1¾in)

Coloured chalk pastels

Scalpel

Facial tissue

Use the pattern above as a guide when you arrange your quilled shapes. The pattern is actual size.

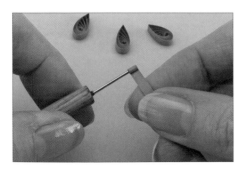

1. Make seven teardrops (as shown on page 47) from pink strips in one matching shade for the petals.

2. Make a peg (see page 47) from a strip in a contrasting shade of pink. Then make two eye shapes (see page 47) from 75mm (3in) lengths of green strip.

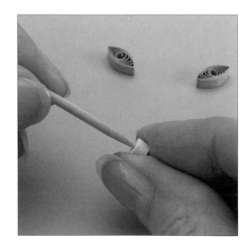

3. Make three triangles (see page 47) from 112mm (4½in) brown strips. Glue them together as above to make a flowerpot. Now glue a brown strip around the edge and snip off the excess.

4. With a pencil and ruler, divide the white paper into five sections. You now need to colour the sections in shades of pink from dark (left) to light (right) using chalk pastels. Use a scalpel to scrape shavings of chalk pastel over one section.

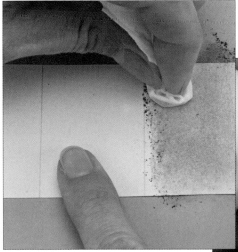

5. Use a facial tissue to rub the chalk pastel shavings into the card. Repeat on the four other sections.

Tip
Your flower petals will look much better if the insides of the teardrops all face the same way.

6. Mark the 74mm (2⁷⁄₈in) point on the shortest side of the blank card and fold it in half. Glue the chalked panel to the front of the card. Now begin assembling the first flower. Position the seven petals, and when you are happy with the arrangement, glue the petals down one at a time.

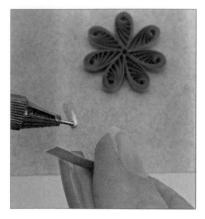

7. Fold the 30mm (1⅜in) green strip in half and glue the sides together to make the stem.

8. Spread a small amount of glue along the edge of the stem.

9. Place the top of the stem between the petals before lowering the whole stem on to the paper.

10. Glue down the flowerpot and both of the leaves. A cocktail stick is useful for positioning small pieces like the leaves.

11. Finally, glue the peg to the centre of the flower. Repeat steps 1 to 3 and 6 to 11 four times to complete the card.

12. Now add the border. Apply glue to the card following the pencil line. This will be neater than trying to apply glue to the strip.

13. Place the brown 2mm (³⁄₃₂in) strip over the glue, taking care to line it up with the bottom of the chalked panel. Trim off the excess strip, cutting it flush to the top of the panel. Glue all six vertical parts of the border in this way. Then attach a strip along the length of the panel at the top and one along the bottom.

A row of flowers creates impact, especially when it is given a bold border. Quilling strips are very useful for making a quick, accurate border. Using 2mm (^{3}/$_{32}$in) strips rather than 3mm (^{1}/$_8$in) will give you a more delicate result.

Your quilling does not have to be completely glued to a background. Here I have made a concertinaed card with flowers that stand proud. Instead of a double thickness strip, I have used a paper stick for the stem to make the flowers more robust. I have also outlined the petals by wrapping a contrasting strip around each teardrop before gluing them all together.

You can adapt this basic design in a variety of ways. One advantage of quilling is that you can take a design and by just halving or doubling the measurements, make a smaller or larger version. The tension will remain the same, it is the length of the strip that governs the size of your design. This window box is simply an extended flowerpot. Just increase the size of the triangles and keep adding more until you achieve the length you want.

Sunflower Girl

This design uses solid coils made from paper strips in a range of different widths. The method is exactly the same for all the coils, it is just that the paper width varies from 2mm ($^3/_{32}$in) to 15mm ($^5/_8$in).

It is worth practising this skill – there is a good quilling tradition whereby you drop the coil several times before achieving ultimate success! Once you have mastered the basic figure, it is fun creating different characters.

A solid coil is really useful for making a face as you do not want a hole in the centre! When it comes to making the arms and legs, I find it easier to start them off by rolling the strips round a long pin. Remove the pin, unroll the paper, then continue rolling with your fingers.

Use the pattern above as a guide when you arrange your quilled shapes. The pattern is actual size.

Tip
Wash your hands before rolling the solid coil to ensure that your sunflower girl does not get a dirty face! Try to handle faces as little as possible as the grease from your hand will easily show on a light-coloured paper.

You will need

Face:
2 pale pink 2mm ($^3/_{32}$in) strips, 450mm (17$^3/_4$in) and 224mm (8$^7/_8$in) long
Dark brown 5mm ($^3/_{16}$in) strip, 70mm (2$^3/_4$in) long
Light brown 1mm ($^1/_{32}$in) strip, 30mm (1$^1/_4$in) long
18 yellow 2mm ($^3/_{32}$in) strips, 56mm (2$^1/_4$in) long

Arms and legs:
2 pale pink 10mm ($^3/_8$in) strips, 45mm (1$^3/_4$in) long
2 pale pink 15mm ($^5/_8$in) strips, 50mm (2in) long

Hands:
2 pale pink 2mm ($^3/_{32}$in) strips, 56mm (2$^1/_4$in) long

Feet:
2 dark green 2mm ($^3/_{32}$in) strips, 56mm (2$^1/_4$in) long

Body:
2 pale green 2mm ($^3/_{32}$in) strips, 450mm (17$^3/_4$in) long
Pale green tissue paper
Dark green 1mm ($^1/_{16}$in) strip, 30mm (1$^1/_4$in) long
2 dark green 2mm ($^3/_{32}$in) strips, 56mm (2$^1/_4$in) long

Quilling tool
Fine black pen
Scissors
Fine-tip glue applicator
Cocktail sticks
Long pin
Florist wire
Ruler
Blank card, 174 x 114mm (7 x 4$^1/_2$in)

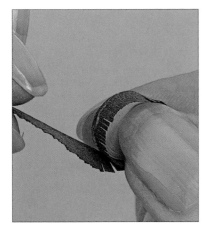

1. To make the face, first roll the 450mm (17¾in) pink strip into a solid coil. Join on the 224mm (8⅞in) strip and continue rolling. Gluing the strips end to end in this way avoids creating a ridge. Now cut a fringe into the dark brown strip and glue it around your solid coil.

2. Fan out the fringing, then make 18 yellow eye shapes. Glue them all the way around the back of the fringing as shown. Allow plenty of time for the glue to dry.

3. Make a spiral from the light brown strip and glue it, a little at a time, around the face to create hair. Then use a fine black pen to draw on her eyes and mouth.

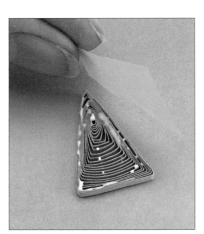

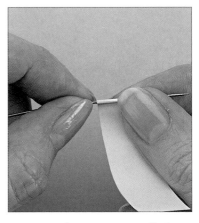

4. For the sunflower girl's body, first join together two pale green 2mm (³/₃₂in) strips and then roll the long strip into a coil. Shape the coil into a teardrop.

5. Now shape the teardrop into a triangle. Apply glue to the back and place the pale green tissue paper over it. Once the glue is dry, trim away any excess tissue paper.

6. To make an arm, roll the 10mm (³/₈in) pink strip around a pin, then remove the pin and re-roll by hand. Repeat to make another arm.

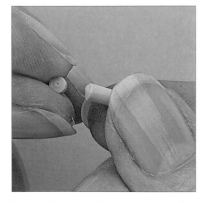  

7. Roll a peg from pale pink 2mm (³/₃₂in) strip for each of her hands.

8. To make the legs, roll each of the 15mm (⁵/₈in) pink strips into pegs. Make two coils from dark green 2mm (³/₃₂in) strip for the feet and squash them flat. Glue the feet to the legs and leave until completely dry.

9. Glue the arms and legs, one at a time, to the back of the body, making sure that the seam of the join on each arm and leg is not visible at the front.

10. Make two small eye shapes using a dark green 2mm (³/₃₂in) strip for each leaf. Now make a spiral from dark green 1mm (¹/₃₂in) strip for the stem. Glue the spiral down the centre of the body and trim off any excess. Next glue on the head and finally, attach each of the leaves. Use a cocktail stick to position the leaves. Allow your sunflower girl to dry before gluing her to the card.

This whimsical flower girl is perfect for wishing someone 'Happy Birthday' or 'Get Well Soon'. Try using other flesh tones for the arms, hands, legs and face. You do not necessarily need to use wide quilling strips for the arms; other kinds of paper will do as long as the paper is thin enough to roll and roughly the same shade as the strips you are using. Envelopes are often good for this purpose.

Left top

Little girls can be dressed in a variety of ways. You can move the hem line up on a dress by making a shorter triangle. Add more quilling at the hem, to create different styles.

Left bottom

Each ballet dancer has a short, square body and a series of teardrops to make a tutu. Note how the arms and legs are the same basic pattern, they are just glued at different angles. Keep practising, girls...

Above

These little figures lend themselves to free-standing cards. Here I have experimented with different kinds of flower girls. You could write a message on the rectangles beneath.

Eyelet Cards

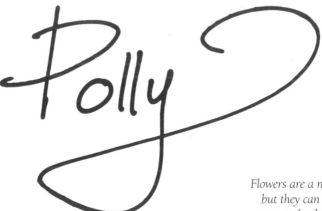

by Polly Pinder

Eyelets were a lovely surprise for me. Having used them years ago in the making of belts and children's gym bags, I never thought that they would become part of the card maker's kit.

We card makers are always looking for innovative ideas to embellish our cards and eyelets certainly fulfil that brief. Made from aluminium, they can be practical, decorative or both. It is difficult to believe that something which requires a thoroughly good hammering can ultimately produce a very delicate and intricate design. The manufacturers have designed additional pieces which lie between the paper and the eyelet, representing anything from a Christmas tree to an open hand, an apple, a snowflake or even a tiny birthday cake with candles. These, combined with the variety of papers and card now available, add a fascinating new dimension to cardmaking.

My daughter said that she thought handmade cards were little works of art in themselves, and I believe she is right. Time, patience and love go into each one and that is why the recipient treasures them. As your cards become ever more professional, do remember to put your name somewhere discreetly so that people appreciate your talents.

I hope you will follow some of the designs in this section and that they will prove an inspiration for you to develop new eyelet ideas of your own.

Polly

Opposite
Flowers are a natural subject for eyelets but they can be put to any number of uses to develop and enhance a design.

Materials

Cards and papers

The range of wonderful cards and papers available to card makers seems to increase yearly, which is great. The card needs to be firm enough to stand on its own when folded. Despite all the hammering required to secure eyelets, they do not seem to distort the card at all. If you like a particular paper, perhaps a mulberry tissue paper or a beautiful handmade paper which lacks the strength to stand on its own, simply glue it on to card. Cut it large enough to make a neat, parallel border going over the fold of the card and on to the back.

Quality magazines are also a good source of paper, but the paper must not be so thin that printed images can be seen through from the back when it is glued down. I have used garden magazines, antique and interior design magazines and seed catalogues for the cards in this book.

The insides of old envelopes were used to create the variety of patterned flowers on page 73. Gift wrap can also be used for backgrounds.

Wallpaper is also very useful. The textured types can be painted with acrylic paint to fit into your colour scheme.

No matter how tight your budget, in our throw-away society there are always plenty of papers that we card makers can recycle.

Eyelets and eyelet tool kit

The eyelet tool kit comprises sturdy piercing tools in different sizes to make the initial hole, an equally sturdy setting tool for pressing the eyelet into the card, a hammer and a cutting mat. Sometimes the piercing tool and setting tool are interchangeable heads which screw into a single handle. These components can be bought separately or as a combined kit. You can buy an eyelet setting mat, but I use an ordinary cutting mat.

Eyelets come in a wide range of colours but if your chosen colour is not within the range, you can always paint them using acrylic paints, tint them with felt-tipped markers or even use nail varnish to achieve a pearlescent effect. You could also dab on a little varnish, then dust the eyelets with fine glitter. If you are making changes to the colour, secure the eyelets in adhesive putty while working on them.

A hammer with piercing and setting tools for attaching eyelets.

Acrylic paint, nail varnish and felt-tipped marker pen can all be used to colour eyelets, which should be secured in adhesive putty when colouring.

Embellishments

You will need a variety of threads and cords. The glittery, metallic embroidery threads are particularly useful; they come in different thicknesses and shades of gold and silver. The plain, brightly coloured embroidery silks and narrow ribbons are also very useful.

Rubber stamps and embossing powder add another aspect to your card design, as do felt-tipped and gel pens.

You can also incorporate photographs into your cards.

Felt-tipped pens, gel pens, photographs, a permanent marker, ribbon, embroidery silks, metallic threads, embossing powder, a rubber stamp and glitter.

Other materials

Cutting implements and accessories You will need a pair of sharp scissors and a good quality craft knife with spare blades. I prefer to use a knife with a strong, steel handle. A circle aperture cutter (rather like compasses with a blade) or curved cuticle scissors are very useful for cutting out circles. A self-healing cutting mat is very important, and you will also need a steel ruler. Decorative craft punches and fancy-edged scissors are invaluable accessories for the card maker.

Glues and sticky tapes I have used glue stick, clear all-purpose glue, ordinary sticky tape, double-sided tape and 3D foam squares.

Drawing materials Tracing paper is necessary for transferring the templates in the book on to your card or paper. You will need an HB pencil and, if the paper is dark, a white pencil. A sharpener and an eraser will be useful. You may also need a pair of compasses or a circle template.

Crimping machine This is used to give a crimped, three-dimensional effect to flat paper. It is useful for adding another texture to your card.

Knitting needle If you are making your own cards, the best implement for scoring prior to folding is a knitting needle. Simply pull it down against your ruler as if you were drawing a line.

Clockwise from top left: craft punches, circle template, crimping machine, double-sided tape and sticky tape, craft knife and blades, metal ruler, 3D foam squares, tracing paper, compasses, fancy-edged craft scissors, cuticle scissors, darning needle for threading ribbon, paper scissors, eraser, all-purpose glue, glue stick, white pencil, HB pencil, circle aperture cutter, pencil sharpener, knitting needle, self-healing cutting mat.

Basic techniques

Eyelets could not be simpler to use and you can always release any pent-up frustration by using the hammer! Be sure to buy the correct sized tools to match your eyelets; if the piercing tool is too large, the set eyelet will not have sufficient grip on the card and the eyelet will fall through.

1. Mark where the eyelets will be on your card.

2. Always work on a cutting or setting mat when attaching eyelets. Open the card flat, hold the piercing tool on one of the marks and hammer. One blow should be enough.

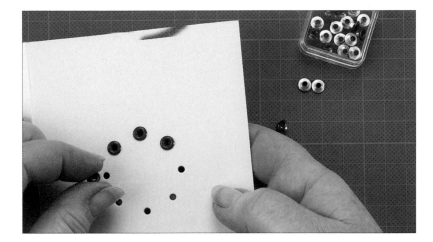

3. Insert the eyelet.

4. Turn the card over and insert the setting tool. One or two knocks with the hammer will curl the tube of the eyelet and press it into the card.

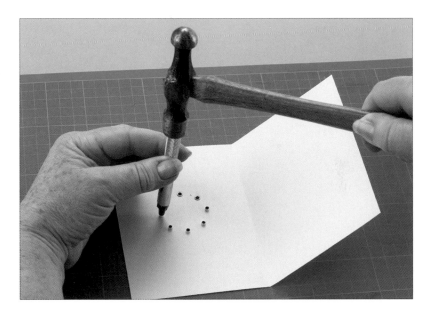

If the eyelet has a decorative piece, lay this over the punched hole before inserting the eyelet.

Floral Glory

Most card makers hoard anything remotely interesting that could enhance their cards or add a touch of originality. The little flowers for this card were punched from used envelopes. Many years ago someone decided to print a simple repeating pattern on the inside of envelopes, to make it impossible to decipher the contents of any letter inside. How useful for us! There are many different patterns which look lovely in an arrangement with plain coloured eyelets of a similar shape.

You will need

White card, 100 x 210mm
(4 x 8½in)

Dark blue mulberry tissue,
90 x 200mm (3½ x 8in)

Cream card, 50 x 200mm
(3½ x 8in)

A variety of used envelopes

Flower eyelets: five cream with
blue centres and two blue
with cream centres

Small cream eyelets

Eyelet tool kit

Flower craft punch

Cutting mat, craft knife
and scissors

White pencil, graphite pencil
and tracing paper

Glue stick

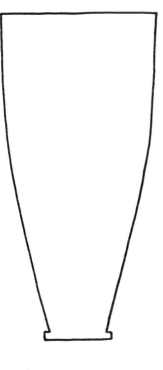

The template for the vase, shown full size.

1. Carefully apply glue stick to one side of the mulberry tissue. Stick the tissue paper on to the card, leaving a neat border all the way round.

70

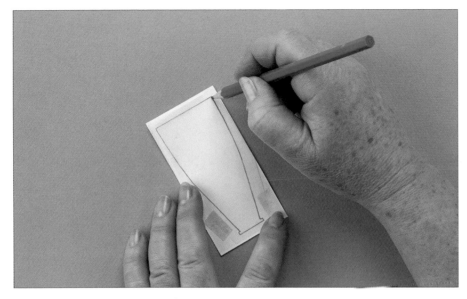

2. Transfer the vase template on to the cream card using tracing paper and a pencil.

3. Punch fifteen flowers with a variety of patterns from your used envelopes.

4. Cut out the cream vase shape and stick it on to your main card, 32mm (1¼in) from the bottom edge, using glue stick. Arrange the paper flowers and flower eyelets. Place the two blue flower eyelets on the vase so that they are not lost on the dark background.

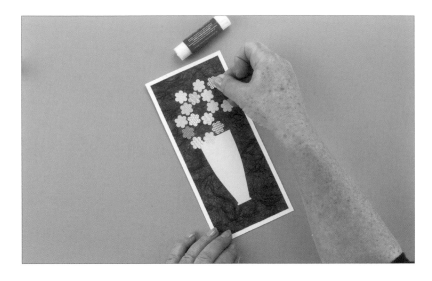

5. When you are happy with the arrangement, remove one paper flower at a time and stick it down using the glue stick.

6. Using the white pencil, mark the centre of each cream flower eyelet. Repeat with the blue flower eyelets using the graphite pencil. Remove the flowers, open the card and, working on the cutting mat, make holes with the eyelet piercing tool over each mark. Make holes for the little cream eyelets in the centre of some of the paper flowers.

7. Position the flowers and push the eyelets through. Turn the card over and, using the setting tool and hammer, set all the eyelets.

Opposite

The finished card. These little flower eyelets, which have a slight sheen, contrast beautifully with the patterned matt finish of the envelope flowers.

*This plant pot was cut from an old gardening magazine. It adds a three-
dimensional effect to the design. The flowers were cut with craft punches, the 'buds'
with an office hole punch.*

Left: All these flowers were cut from old gardening magazines using three flower punches. The stalks were cut from green card and coloured with a green felt-tipped pen to give slight variation. Right: The purple vase was scanned from an old magazine, then coloured on the computer. The flower heads, cut with a craft punch, and fringed mat are made from handmade Indian tissue paper.

Sunflower

Eyelets make perfect centres for sunflowers; they can graphically represent all those hundreds of seeds. This design is a simple concept; the interest lies in the contrast between the large, bright yellow petals and the smaller patterned leaves, cut from an old seed catalogue. Having drawn the petals at different angles, the yellow card was then put through a crimping machine. This gave a subtly different direction to each petal.

You will need
Tracing paper and pencil

Orange card blank,
140 x 190mm (5½ x 7½in)

Yellow card 130 x 200mm
(5 x 8in)

Brown card 70mm
(3in) square

Two strips of pale green paper
20 x 150mm (¾ x 6in)

Old seed catalogues for varied
leaf patterns

Fine black felt-tipped pen

Crimping machine

Compasses

Twenty-one gold coloured
eyelets and eyelet tool kit

Craft knife, cutting mat and
metal ruler

Circle aperture cutter and
scissors

Clear all-purpose glue and
glue stick

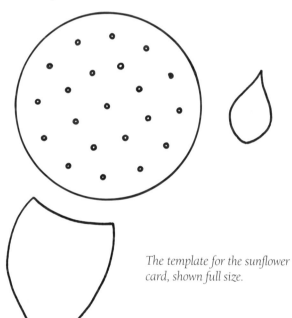

The template for the sunflower card, shown full size.

1. Transfer twelve petals at different angles on to the yellow card. Put the card through the crimping machine, then cut the petals out.

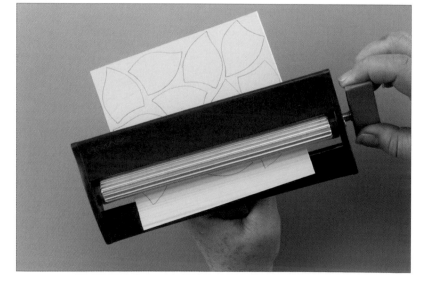

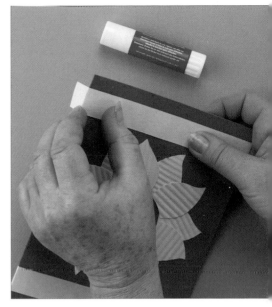

2. Draw a circle in the centre of the orange card blank, slightly smaller than the flower centre (see template).

3. Stick the green strips of paper on to the card 10mm (³⁄₈in) from the top and bottom edges. Bend the overlap round the back to give a neat finish to the fold of the card.

4. Transfer the small leaf shape on to a spare piece of yellow card. Carefully cut the leaf out with your craft knife and use the opening as a template. Using the black felt-tipped pen, draw the leaf eighteen times on the various pieces of patterned leaf paper.

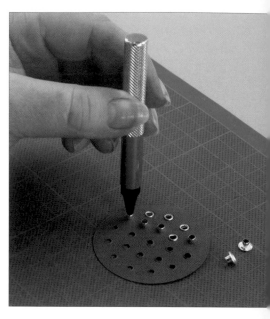

5. Cut the leaves out, cutting away the black pen line. Arrange the leaves on the green strips, the nine on the top strip pointing in the opposite direction to those on the bottom strip. Stick them down using glue stick.

6. Transfer the circle, including the dots, on to the brown card, then carefully cut it out (use your circle aperture cutter if you have one). Use the eyelet piercing tool to make holes as indicated by the dots. Put the eyelets through the holes and set them.

7. Run a line of clear glue round the underside of the flower centre, then position it to cover the inner edges of the petals.

The finished card. Growing sunflowers has become very popular. This would make a nice 'congratulations' card when someone's sunflower has reached dizzy heights, as they often do! It would also make a great card for someone with a summer birthday.

The eyelets for this flower have been painted and arranged differently. The petals have been cut from old seed catalogues, like the leaves on the project card.

Felt-tipped pens were used to colour the petals of these little sunflowers, and to colour the eyelets. The centres were made separately, then stuck on to the flowers.

This flower was cut from mulberry paper – tissue paper with threads of silk running through it.
The round eyelet secures four circles with finely cut edges.

Quick Parchment Cards

by Janet Wilson

The cards in this section feature a cross between simple embossing techniques and paper pricking borrowed from the original, more time-consuming parchment art form. This section looks at making parchment cards using a basic kit and three-step stencils and suggests ways of mounting your finished pieces as attractive cards. You will learn how to colour the parchment paper prior to embossing as well as how to spot colour areas of the embossed project, using permanent marker pens and coloured pencils. Ideas for freehand decoration of the projects are shown, and how you can devise your own designs by using only parts of the stencils.

For the more adventurous, I suggest more advanced ways of using the stencils, and introduce a couple of basic decorative techniques from the original parchment art form.

If you enjoy all the projects and really get hooked, perhaps you will want to go further and try your hand at the original, ancient art of making parchment cards. In the meantime, enjoy using these simple techniques to make beautiful handmade cards.

Opposite

A selection of cards showing the many different ways the stencils can be used. Embossing, pricking and colouring are combined with decorative techniques borrowed from the original parchment art form.

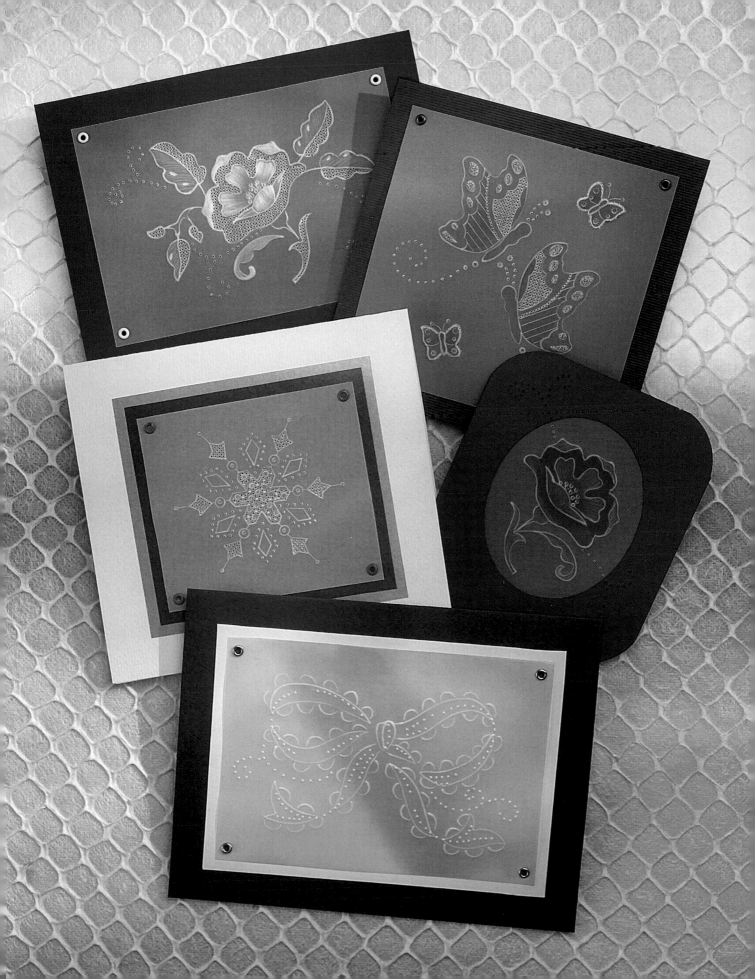

Materials

The basic kit

All the cards in this book were made using a kit produced by Fiskars, plus a few other items. The kit includes:

Mini Shapeboss base This is used in conjunction with duo embossing stencils, meaning that you do not need a light box. The parchamoré system described below has been created to fit this base.

Parchamoré crafting system comprising:

Two sets of three-step stencils, the bow and the rose These are numbered stencils used in order for embossing and perforating designs.

Dual-tip large ball embossing and perforating tool For embossing and perforating areas of the work.

Combined perforating and embossing mat This fits on to the Mini Shapeboss base.

White pencil Used to colour areas of the designs as desired.

160gsm parchment paper I find this too thick and prefer to use a normal weight parchment, which gives a better finish.

Cards and envelopes These are included in the kit so that you can complete projects without having to buy additional materials.

The three-step stencils are numbered 1/3, 2/3 and 3/3 so that you emboss and paper prick the design in the correct order.

Other essentials

Dual-tip medium/small ball embossing tool I prefer to use the medium ball tool rather than the large one that comes with the kit as it produces a more delicate line.

Additional stencils You can buy many other stencils as well as those found in the kit.

140gsm parchment paper This has been used throughout the book. The maximum width of parchment that can be used on the Mini Shapeboss base is 16cm (6¼in).

A5 piece of 3mm deep fun foam This is used as a mat with the Puerto Rican cutting tools. It can also be used as a perforating mat if you do not want to keep taking the combined mat off the base.

Low tack tape Used to attach the parchment to the combined mat to keep it in place when changing stencils.

Double-sided tape Used to attach layers of paper or card to the base card. Do not use it for attaching parchment, as it will show.

The parchamoré crafting system with the Mini Shapeboss base and additional stencils.

Permanent spray adhesive This can also be used for attaching paper or card to the base card. Do not use it to attach parchment.

Beeswax block Sometimes the embossing tool does not move smoothly over the parchment. Rubbing it across the surface of a beeswax block (or the greasy patch on your chin!) makes it glide easily.

Plastic cutting ruler with a grid Mine has a 0.5cm ($^3/_{16}$in) grid. This makes cutting borders around layers easier.

Craft knife and cutting mat For cutting parchment, paper and card.

Optionals

South American style hard embossing mat This mat really improves your embossing and is essential if you want to use an estralina tool.

Large and small Brazilian estralina This tool was originally used only in Southern Brazil and was a mini drillhead pushed into a mechanical pencil. After my Brazilian colleague and I introduced it to the rest of the world, several companies have brought out their own versions with names such as 'star' or 'sun tool'.

Puerto Rican cutting tools I discovered these in 1986 when I started learning parchment art. Use them on a fun foam mat, just piercing the surface rather than pushing them right down. I have used a medium scallop tool in the 'Roses are Red' project.

Masking tape Used for making the home-made perforating grid (see page 87) and for securing parchment to the grid.

Medium circle hand punch Used for punching holes for eyelets.

Circle aperture cutter Used for making aperture cards into which parchment projects can be mounted.

Corner rounder scissors These are the easiest way to make rounded corners on cards or layers.

Craft punches I use various styles of main design and corner punches.

Index tabs These are low tack tabs with a coloured end, ideal for keeping stencils or projects in place.

Mini clips These ultra-mini bulldog clips are wonderful for holding pieces of paper together, (e.g. a pattern with card or parchment) while you cut a piece to size.

Tweezers Useful for picking up eyelets and small punched shapes.

Super non-spray adhesive This tape is excellent for attaching punched shapes. Place the shape on to the sticky side, which is covered with tiny glue dots. Roll the tape back, unroll it, peel off the shape and attach.

Clockwise from the top: Puerto Rican scallop and straight edge cutting tools, craft knife, cutting mat, rulers, spray adhesive, masking tape, fun foam mat, hard embossing mat, brass mesh perforating grid (see page 9), strong scissors, medium circle hand punch (lavender handles), aperture cutter, corner rounder scissors, photo corner punch, star and snowflake punches, beeswax block, index tabs, mini clips, tweezers, small and large estralina tools. Centre: double-sided tape, low tack tape (green in middle) and super non-spray adhesive.

Embellishments

Permanent markers These dry quickly on parchment and the ones I used are available in pastel colours, ideal for parchment projects.

Paint brush Use a flat brush to blend dark and pale shades of permanent marker colours.

Good quality coloured pencils and a blender pencil Artist quality pencils are softer, well pigmented and last a long time. Some ranges are available as individual pencils. A blender pencil is used to blend colours for a professional finish.

Plastic eraser If you have put too much coloured pencil on your work, or gone over the edges, use this before the blender pencil.

Eyelet kit All adhesives show on parchment, and using eyelets is a decorative way to attach projects to layers and/or the base card. The hammer I use has a piercing tool inside the handle, and a setting tool inside that. The piercing tool must never be used with the setting tool inside, or the screw threads will be damaged. Use a setting mat when setting eyelets, as the tool will damage a cutting mat.

Dye inkpads The ink from these can be applied to the back of parchment using a cosmetic sponge, and dries quickly.

Clockwise from the top: permanent marker pens, paint brush, appliqué glue, cosmetic sponges, dye inkpads, plastic eraser, blender pencil, eraser pencil, coloured pencils, eyelet setting mat, hammer plus two setting tools, gold thread, cotton bud. Centre: eyelets in various colours and gold beads.

Appliqué glue Available in many colours and in metallic or glitter effects. Allow it to dry for at least thirty minutes.

Metallic embroidery thread Used to sew parchment projects to layers or the base card. Use the thread that is sold on bobbins, which comes in many metallic as well as hologram colours.

Beads Use these with metallic thread to add chic to projects.

Card and paper

Darker colours work best behind parchment projects. These can then be mounted on to paler coloured card. All adhesives show on parchment, so mount your work using photo corner punches or eyelets.

Paper, card and vellum can all be used to create beautiful cards using quick parchment techniques.

Home-made perforating grid

The perforating grid is used for Argentinian decorative perforating techniques featured in some of the projects where a regular pattern is required. You can make your own using brass mesh and masking tape.

You will need

Brass mesh, gauge 7 holes per cm ($^3/_8$in)

Masking tape 2.5cm (1in) wide

Large 6mm ($^1/_4$in) single hole punch

Black permanent marker

Mat from the parchamoré system

Ruler

Strong scissors

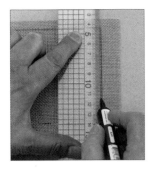

1. Use the marker to draw a rectangle 12 x 16cm (4¾ x 6¼in) on the brass mesh. Cut it out using the strong scissors.

2. Place a piece of masking tape on one of the long sides of the mesh so that the straight edge of the tape is on the third line from the edge of the mesh. Fold the tape in half and position the other edge in alignment with the piece on the front.

3. Repeat this for the other long side and trim any excess masking tape from the ends.

4. On one of the short sides of the mesh, place a piece of masking tape on the third line from the edge of the mesh and stick a second piece of tape exactly behind it. Repeat for the other short side.

5. Place the mat from the parchamoré crafting system on to the mesh and mark where the holes are on the short taped sides.

6. Punch through the tape with the single hole punch to make the holes.

7. The perforating grid now fits on to the Mini Shapeboss base. Place the project on the grid, secure with masking tape and use the perforating tool vertically to perforate through the holes in the relevant areas of the project.

Basic techniques

Making a control piece

The stencils used throughout this section are three-step stencils, two of which are normally for embossing. The third may have a combination of further embossing and perforating work, or may be solely for perforating. I recommend that you make what I call a control piece for each of the sets of stencils you purchase and keep it with the stencils. The control piece shows all the embossing and perforating areas contained on the three-step stencils. When you have made it, you can decide which lines you need not emboss for your project and which parts of the perforating you want to use or leave out. This piece is also of great assistance when you want to change the direction of, say, a piece of ribbon when you start experimenting with more advanced projects using the stencils.

This demonstration shows you how to make a control piece using the bow stencils.

You will need

Basic kit plus Bow three-step stencil

Parchment paper 14.5 x 9.8cm (5¾ x 3⅞in)

Low tack tape

Dual-tip medium/small ball embossing tool

South American style hard embossing mat

Ruler with a grid

Dye inkpads and cosmetic sponges

Scrap card

Permanent markers

Flat no. 4 paint brush

Coloured pencils and blender pencil

Plastic eraser

Large estralina

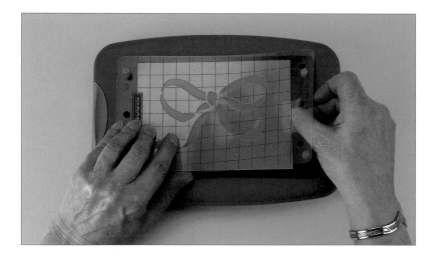

1. Position a piece of parchment underneath stencil 1 and tape it to the mat using low tack tape. You can turn the base when embossing or perforating so that it is in the best position for you.

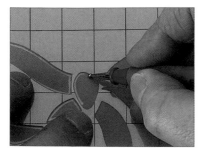

2. Emboss the areas on stencil 1 using the medium embossing tool. Plastic stencils are prone to move while you are working, so keep your fingers on the stencil to hold it still.

Tip

If you are using normal weight parchment, you do not have to press hard when embossing. Apply a similar pressure to that which you would use with a pencil.

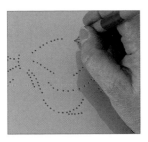

3. Emboss the areas on stencil 2 in the same way.

4. Perforate with stencil 3 using the perforating tool. Always keep the tool upright when perforating.

The finished control piece. Keep this with the three-step stencils so that you can see at a glance what effects are produced by all the stencils.

Tip

When using the perforating tool, you only need to break the surface of the paper. If you push the tool down too far it will 'bruise' the parchment, leaving a white mark, and you will also distort the hole on the stencil.

Stippling and using white pencil

Normally the control piece would be kept for a reference, but here I have decorated it in order to demonstrate two further techniques.

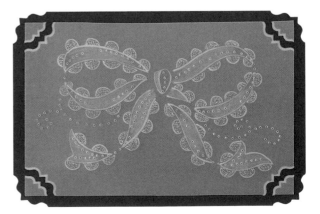

1. Put the parchment on the hard embossing mat or a cutting mat and using the perforating tool, stipple the half-moons along the ribbon edge. Gently bounce the tool up and down.

2. Turn the parchment over and using a white pencil, shade the ribbon area. This will give the design light.

The finished piece. To mount the project, I cut a piece of dark paper measuring 6mm (¼in) more all round than the parchment. A photo corner punch was used on each corner and the parchment was slipped in and secured using small pieces of sticky tape on the back. Spray adhesive or double-sided tape could be used to adhere this layer to the base card.

Cross hatching

This method of decorating parchment projects is used in South America. It is easy to do and the resulting pattern can be decorated in various ways. I recommend using a hard embossing mat for this work.

1. Working on the back of the parchment and using a ruler with a grid and the perforating tool, emboss parallel lines across the ribbon. Do not press too hard.

2. Turn the parchment round and starting in the middle, cross hatch with lines at right angles to the first lines. The grid on the ruler will help.

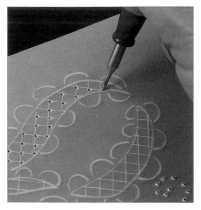

3. Place the parchment, right side up on the perforating mat and use the perforating tool to make holes where the lines cross.

4. Turn the parchment over. Using the embossing tool, rub each of the half moons with a back and forth motion.

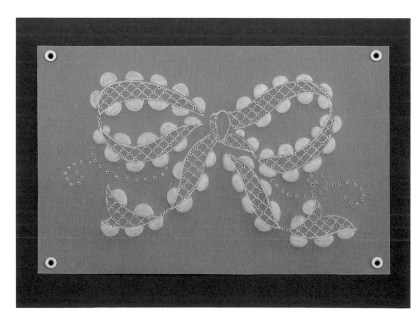

The finished piece. This time the parchment project has been attached to the base card using eyelets. Parchment work shows to better advantage on a dark background like this.

Colouring parchment

Sometimes you may want to use coloured parchment or add colour to areas of the design to give a different effect to your work. Here are some methods that I use.

Using inkpads

The ink from dye inkpads dries fairly quickly, and is easily applied to the back of the parchment using a cosmetic sponge. You can make the colour paler by wiping off excess ink. Check what the colours look like from the right side of the work.

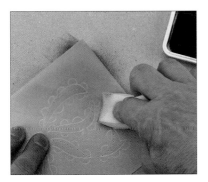

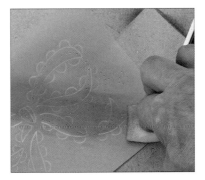

1. Place the parchment face down on a scrap of card. Using a cosmetic sponge, dab on blue ink. Any excess ink can be wiped off using a clean sponge.

2. Dab on red ink using a fresh sponge. It is a good idea to label your sponges with the ink colour so that you do not mix them up!

The finished card. I have added a third colour, then mounted the project on to a pale coloured layer, which shows the coloured parchment better, and attached it to the base card using eyelets.

Spot colouring

This is another easy way of adding a little colour. I use permanent markers as they dry quickly. The colour is applied to the back of the project so remember to check the appearance from the front, which will be different.

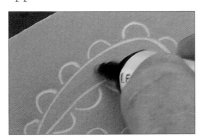

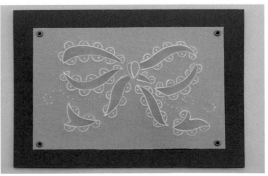

1. Place the parchment face down. Using a pale blue permanent marker, colour some of the ribbon.

2. Add dark blue and before the ink dries, blend the colours together using a flat no. 4 paint brush.

The finished card is attached to a dark, toning coloured base card using eyelets.

Colouring with pencils

Adding colour to your projects using coloured pencils is the method favoured in South America and some delightful effects can be achieved quite simply. Apply light strokes of the pencil to the back of the parchment, starting with the palest and moving on to darker colours. Check the appearance from the front. Any excess colour can be removed with a plastic eraser. After that you can use the blender pencil to blend colours. This does tend to make colours slightly darker.

1. Use a pale blue coloured pencil first.

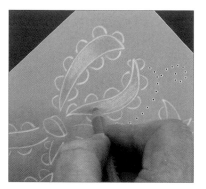

2. Then use a dark blue pencil, overlapping the pale blue slightly.

Tip
You can always rub out mistakes with a plastic eraser.

3. Use a blender pencil over the whole area to smooth out the pencil marks.

4. On the hard embossing mat, use the large estralina on the back of the parchment to make a circle in each half-moon.

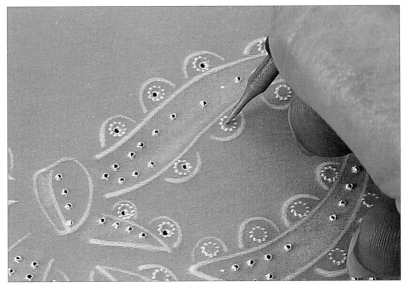

5. Lay the parchment, wrong side up, on to stencil 3 and pierce the pattern in the ribbons using the perforating tool.

6. Turn the parchment the right side up and pierce a hole in the middle of each estralina circle.

The finished card

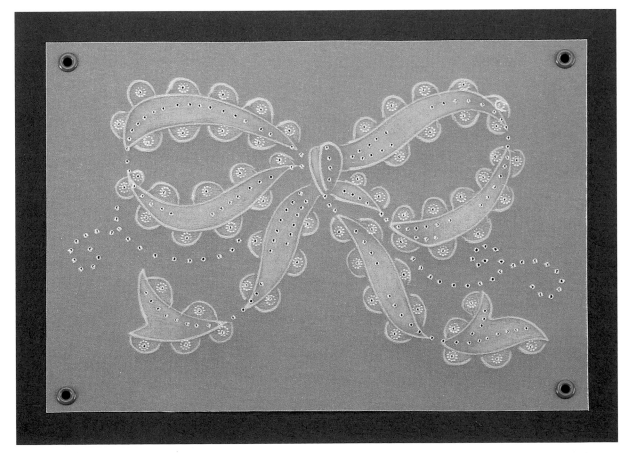

Roses are Red

In this project you will see how to use a Puerto Rican cutting tool to make a scalloped edge. This project also shows you how to sew the parchment project on to a card using metallic thread, and how to incorporate beads. Only part of the stencil has been used.

You will need

Basic kit and Rose three-step stencil

Dual-tip medium/small ball embossing tool

Large and small estralinas

Puerto Rican scallop cutting tool

Fun foam mat

South American style hard embossing mat

A5 parchment paper

Coloured pencils: three shades of red and three shades of green

White pencil and plastic eraser

A4 and A5 red card

Gold metallic thread and needle

Double-sided tape

Low tack tape

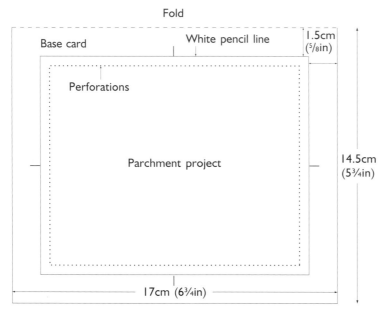

Fold

Base card

White pencil line

1.5cm (⁵⁄₈in)

Perforations

Parchment project

14.5cm (5¾in)

17cm (6¾in)

The pattern for the card shown half size, with measurements marked full size. Enlarge on a photocopier.

1. Place stencil 1 on the base with the trade name to the left and the pegs on the right. Secure the parchment to the mat using low tack tape. Emboss the rose design and some of the leaves using the medium embossing tool.

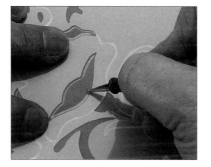

2. Emboss stencil 2 in the same way.

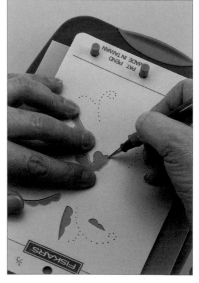

3. Emboss stencil 3.

4. Place stencil 3 on the fun foam mat, lay the parchment on top and perforate the curlicues in the correct areas.

5. Use the pencils to colour the rose on the back of the parchment: the palest shades first, then the mid-tones.

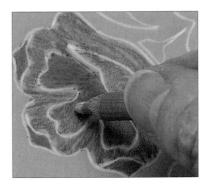

6. Apply the darkest shade of red, then use the blender pencil to merge the colours.

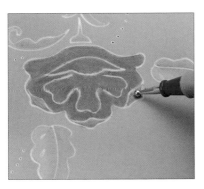

7. Colour the green areas in the same way. Still working on the back of the parchment, emboss the petal tips using the large ball tool so that they turn pale pink.

8. Working on the right side of the parchment, emboss the tops of the inner petals.

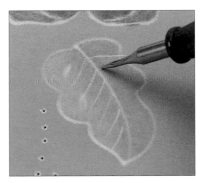

9. On the back, use the perforating tool to draw the veins of the leaves.

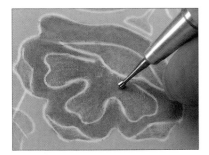

10. Also on the back, use the small estralina to emboss the flower anthers.

11. Place the work right side up on the fun foam mat and perforate along the central vein of the leaf using the perforating tool.

12. Place the parchment right side up on the full-sized pattern. Draw in the white pencil line as marked and pierce along the perforations to create a sewing line.

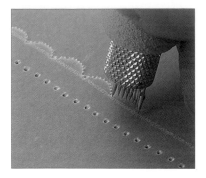

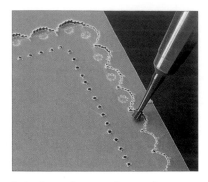

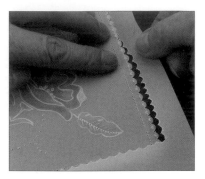

13. Lay the parchment right side up on the fun foam mat and use the Puerto Rican cutting tool to cut scalloped edges, lining up the two outermost needles with the white line. Rub out the white line using a plastic eraser.

14. Lay the work on the hard embossing mat, wrong side up. Use the large estralina along the scalloped edges as shown.

15. Carefully pull the edges away from the finished parchment project, tearing along the scalloped edge.

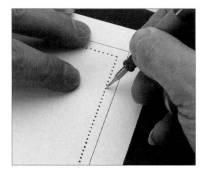

16. Fold the A4 red card in half and lay it on the pattern, matching the fold to the fold line on the pattern. Cut this base card to size (see page 30). Perforate the sewing line again, using the same holes you pierced on the parchment.

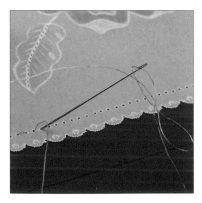

17. Sew the parchment to the card using gold metallic thread. Secure the start and end of the thread to the inside front of the card using double-sided tape.

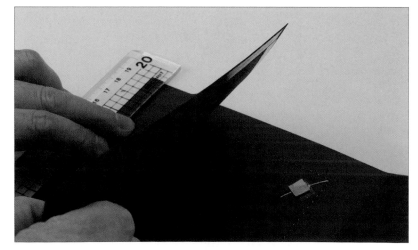

18. To make the neatener, cut a rectangle 12.5 x 15.3cm (5 x 6in) from A5 card. Use double-sided tape to attach it to the inside front of the card to hide the stitching on the back.

The finished card has an elegant simplicity. A craft sticker greeting can be added on the lower left-hand side of the rose.

The stencil has been reversed to create the top rose, whilst the lower one uses it the right way round. The roses have been coloured using various shades of yellow and the edges were cut using a Puerto Rican chevron cutting tool and decorated using an estralina. The project was sewn on to the base card using gold metallic thread.

Top: The red rose has been mounted in an aperture card as shown in the Snowflakes project. Centre: Embossing, the perforating grid and white pencil have been used for a simple but striking effect. Bottom: This example uses the whole of the template. Embossing and perforating techniques have been used without further decoration.

Silk Ribbon Cards

by Ann Cox

Experimenting and developing new ideas is enormous fun, but when I started this section I had absolutely no idea the hours of pleasure I would have doing it. I was allowed to develop ideas and techniques from silk ribbon embroidery and simplify the methods of working to make them suitable for cardmaking. The projects are small and therefore quick to work, so why spend hours searching for a card with that extra something when you can create one that is original and really personal?

First and foremost I am a silk ribbon embroidery designer and without doubt this is my first love. I only work with silk – its characteristics make it easy and quick for the embroiderer to shape each individual stitch. The only stitches I have worked for the cards in this section are ribbon stitch, straight stitch and gathering stitch in ribbon and couching and fly stitch in thread, but I have used new and different techniques to create this wide variety of flowers for you to choose from. All of these cards work on both fabric and card and you do not need to use an embroidery hoop. I also show you how to paint the ribbon to increase the range of flowers that can be worked.

At the start, make sure you have an envelope to fit the finished card. It is infuriating when finished to find there is no envelope to fit. Keep the project simple – avoid having too many fussy bits and pieces and above all keep the work impeccably clean.

As you turn the pages of this book I hope you will be tempted. There are lots of new ideas and techniques to make card making easier and give a more professional finish. Use these ideas and never be afraid to experiment to create your own original cards.

Happy sewing!

Thread stitches

Couching: A single strand of toning thread is used to secure another thread in place. This is useful when working curved stems.

Fly stitch: This is a single open looped stitch similar to a lazy daisy stitch. It is often worked as a calyx for flowers such as rosebuds.

Opposite
A selection of the beautiful cards that can be made by embroidering with silk ribbon without using an embroidery hoop.

Materials

Silk ribbons

Pure silk is soft and fine, and when woven into ribbon, it allows the embroiderer to create stitches that are quite unique – impossible to obtain using any other fibre. Working with short lengths – no more than 33cm (13in) – the ribbon is threaded on to a needle and stitched using traditional embroidery stitches just like an embroidery thread. Ribbon is available in four widths: 2mm ($^1/_{16}$in), 4mm ($^1/_8$in), 7mm ($^1/_4$in) and 13mm ($^1/_2$in). Every stitch worked in ribbon will cover a much bigger area than a thread stitch. Ribbon is perfect for working through card as well as fabric. Silk is a natural fibre, making it easy to paint both before and after it has been embroidered to add a subtle depth and quality to the work. Never waste off-cuts; 5cm (2in) of ribbon will make a rosebud or leaf, and it may be just the shade you need to finish a project.

Needles and pins stored in a piece of sponge, on a foam mat used for pricking.

Pins and needles

Chenille needles with their sharp point and large eye are used to embroider silk ribbon and the size of needle used is critical. The hole made must be large enough for the ribbon to pass through without damaging the silk but small enough to allow control of the ribbon on the front. The largest size 13 needle is used for 13mm ($^1/_2$in) ribbon, size 18 for both 7mm ($^1/_4$in) and 4mm ($^1/_8$in), a small size 24 for the 2mm ($^1/_{16}$in) ribbon and a crewel size 8 for embroidery threads. A mapping pin and a few glass-headed pins are also needed.

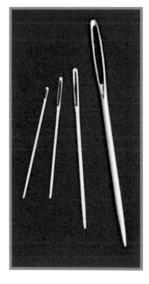

Card and fabric

Card and fabric can be smooth, textured, matt or shiny. Both are available in a limitless variety of colours, sometimes a single colour, sometimes shadowed or patterned. Whichever fabric you choose, it needs to be firm and not too loose a weave, since only small pieces are used and the fabric must be able to support the stitches. Avoid thick fabric as it will create too much bulk in the card. Choose card and/or fabric backgrounds to complement each other and the embroidery and avoid creating a 'busy' card with too many textures and colours.

To make life easy, store card on its end so that it is easy to pick a colour and keep all card off-cuts the same way, but in a separate box. Collect interesting pieces of fabric, no matter how small, but keep them flat.

Tip
When cutting card, place it on a different coloured card, as this will show up the cutting edge.

Card and fabric suitable for silk ribbon embroidery.

Silk painting equipment

Lightly painting a ribbon to alter the tone will bring the finished piece to life. I use silk paint, which is washable if iron fixed, to shade the ribbons and frequently the background fabric. I mix all colours on a kitchen tile from only yellow, blue, red and magenta paints. Paints can be applied using brushes or sponges, or the ribbon can be dropped in the paint on the tile for a patchy effect. I use watercolours to paint card and also at times background fabric, since you will not need to wash a greetings card so colour-fastness is not an issue.

Watercolour paints, silk paints, brushes, a kitchen tile for mixing, a sponge, sponge-painted card and a natural sponge.

Threads

You will need a selection of stranded embroidery threads to anchor ribbons to the fabric, to make a frame for the embroidery or for gathering. Metallic threads can add something special to a design. The small running stitches used to gather ribbon should always match the colour of the ribbon. I also like to use coton à broder or cotton perle in a mixture of greens and a variety of thicknesses for stitching stems. Garden string can be used to create the branches of trees for some designs.

Other materials

I cut all my own cards to the size I require and a good craft knife, preferably with a retractable blade, is essential. Always use a cutting mat or board to prevent damage to work surfaces and blunting the blade and use a small foam mat on which to prick through designs. You will also need a metal ruler, a plastic ruler, a fine sharp pencil, small sharp scissors, paper scissors, a knitting needle, glue stick, a little PVA glue, a small pot of water with a lid to clean brushes, and some kitchen towel. A good quality paper trimmer, not essential but extremely useful, will enable you to cut card accurately and quickly, giving you more time for the fun part of card making. Similarly a pair of fancy-edged scissors will increase the range of finishes you can achieve, as will some glitter.

A pot of water, PVA glue, tweezers, a cutting mat, metal ruler, adhesive putty, glue stick, knitting needle, craft knife, pencil, eraser, syringe for silicone sealant, kitchen paper, fancy-edged, paper and fine scissors and glitter dust.

Silicone sealant

A card is often given an added quality if the embroidery is slightly raised from the base card and to do this I use a clear silicone sealant, available in most hardware stores. It is economical to buy and easy to use. I fill a small syringe so that I can position fine lines easily, and they dry quickly and without any mess. When it is not in use, cover the end with a small piece of adhesive putty to prevent the silicone solidifying in the syringe. Should this happen, either use a needle or tweezers to pull the solid piece out of the end or pull out the plunger and use a small spatula to remove the silicone. Small tubes of silicone are available but I find they produce far too much sealant at a time.

Below: silicone sealant in a gun, as it is bought from hardware stores.

Single Rose

This single rose, worked in 7mm (¼in) silk ribbon is a perfect project for your first silk ribbon card. It can be worked in any colour you choose, but using the two shades: pink (08) and pale pink (05) as I have here will bring the rose to life.

The techniques you will be guided through form the basis for many other cards as well. You will learn how to cut the card and secure fabric in the aperture so that no embroidery hoop is needed. I also show you a quick and easy way to anchor the ribbon (for cardmaking only) and how, with care, to embroider perfect petals to create a rose. Finally there are the vital finer points such as the thorns and kinking the stem, the bow and assembling the card for that professional finish. Have fun and experiment: try changing the colour of the ribbons or card or the size of the aperture and soon every card you create will be unique – one for every occasion.

You will need

Two sheets of red card, 26 x 13cm (10¼ x 5in) and 12cm (4¾in) square

Black linen, 5 x 11cm (2 x 4¼in)

Craft knife, cutting mat, metal ruler and knitting needle

Glue stick

Plastic ruler and pencil

Foam mat

Glass-headed pins and a mapping pin

Needles: two size 18 (medium) chenille for ribbons; a crewel size 8 for embroidery threads

7mm (¼in) silk ribbon: 25cm (10in) each of pink (08), pale pink (05) and deep moss (72)

4mm (⅛in) silk ribbon: 25cm (10in) each of pale pink (05) and deep moss (72)

Toning stranded embroidery threads

Clear silicone sealant

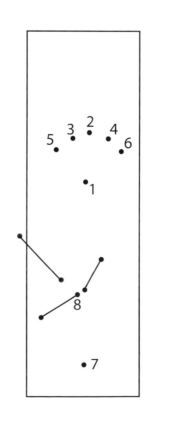

Tip
Always cut silk ribbon at an angle to prevent fraying and make threading a needle easier.

The pattern for the Single Rose card. Photocopy it to make a template.

1. Use a metal ruler and a knitting needle to score and fold the red card in half. Measure and draw a 2.9 x 9.6cm (1⅛ x 3¾in) aperture in the single square of red card. Cut it out using a craft knife and cutting mat.

2. Reduce the width and length of the cutout panel by about 3mm (⅛in).

3. Working on the back of the red card square, apply glue stick round the aperture, taking care not to get glue on the cut edges. Lay the black linen over it and stretch it over the aperture by passing a plastic ruler across the fabric.

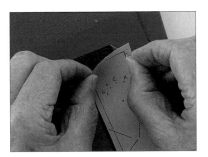

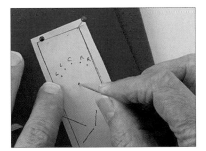

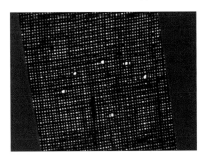

4. Place the card face up on the foam mat and use glass-headed pins to fix the template over the aperture.

5. Now use a size 18 chenille needle to prick through the dots on the template.

The holes made in the linen by the needle in step 5 are clearly visible. It is not necessary to mark them with chalk as this is such a small project.

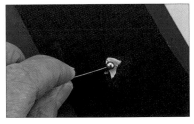

6. Thread the 7mm (¼in) pink ribbon on the needle, then, working on the right side, take the tail end down through hole 1 in the fabric.

7. Always anchor ribbon on the wrong side behind the stitch to be worked, and when finishing off. Apply a little glue stick to the back of the fabric and use a glass-headed pin to smooth down the tail end of the ribbon to secure it.

Tip
Using the eye end of another needle, stroke the underside of the ribbon to straighten and position it before stitching.

 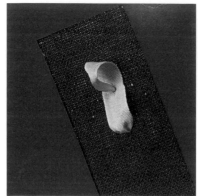 

8. Turn the card face up, lay the ribbon (with a slight lift) over hole 2, then take the needle and ribbon down through the centre of the ribbon and hole 2.

9. Start to pull the ribbon carefully through itself and the fabric...

10. . . . until the petal is formed. Do not pull it too tight or the shape will be lost. This is centre ribbon stitch.

Tip
To shape the petals, use the eye of a second needle the same size as the one used to embroider the ribbon.

11. Bring the ribbon up carefully at 1 and lay it over the first stitch but this time take the needle down through the left-hand edge of the ribbon at 3 and place the eye end of a second needle in the loop to pull the ribbon over. This is a left ribbon stitch.

12. Pull the ribbon firmly over this needle, keeping it in place. Bring the first needle up again at 1 then remove the second needle.

13. Repeat steps 11 and 12 for the third petal, but this time take the needle down through the right-hand edge of the ribbon at 4. This is a right ribbon stitch. Fasten off at the back with a touch of the glue stick as before.

14. Anchor a length of 7mm (¼in) pale pink ribbon at 1, lay the ribbon over the left petal, then work a left ribbon stitch at 5 and a right ribbon stitch at 6. Fasten off as before.

15. Using two strands of green embroidery thread and a crewel size 8 needle, work a straight stitch stem, coming up at 1 and down at 7. Bring the thread up just to the right-hand side of the stem, 7mm (¼in) up from the bottom.

Tip
Avoid bringing the needle up through ribbon on the back of the work, as it will destroy the stitches previously worked.

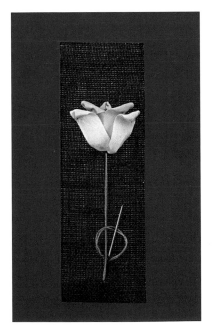

16. Take the thread over then under the stem and back down the same hole to make a loop. Now bring the needle back up through the loop.

17. Pull the stitch tight to create a thorn and a kink in the stem, then take the needle down to make a tiny chain stitch and complete the stitch.

18. Next work a short straight stitch to create a leaf spur, then add two more thorns up the stem.

19. Using 4mm (⅛in) deep moss ribbon, work a left, right and centre ribbon stitch to form the calyx. Anchor the 7mm (¼in) deep moss ribbon at 8 and work three centre ribbon stitches to form the leaves. Work the middle leaf through the card as shown.

Tip
The piece of card fixed behind the aperture takes up the tension of the fabric and should be added to all cards with fabric in an aperture.

20. Use a mapping pin to make two holes in the card 15mm (⅝in) from the left-hand side, 6mm (⁷⁄₁₆in) down from the top and up from the bottom. Use the 4mm (⅛in) pale pink ribbon to lay in a straight stitch, anchoring each end on the back of the card with a touch of glue stick.

21. Tie a bow with the rest of the 4mm (⅛in) pale pink ribbon, then use a single strand of pink thread to anchor the bow through the ribbon and the card.

Tip
It is easier to position a bow with streamers if it is tied separately and then anchored with a thread.

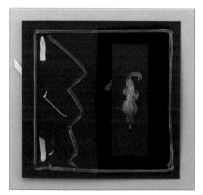

22. Glue the small piece of red card from step 2 on the back of the embroidery, then apply strips of silicone sealant as shown.

23. Place the embroidered panel neatly in the centre of the folded card blank, then use a ruler to level the card on the sealant. The sealant will ensure that the panel sticks firmly to the card but is slightly raised from it.

The finished card. This is a beautiful greetings card, just perfect for any special occasion. You could change the colours of the rose and card, maybe to match a bride's colours or a particular anniversary. You could also use the design to make a box of notelets, place name cards for a dinner party, a panel to go on the top of a pretty box or a gift tag as shown below.

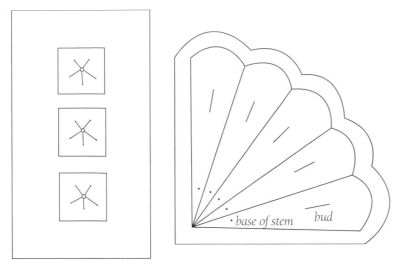

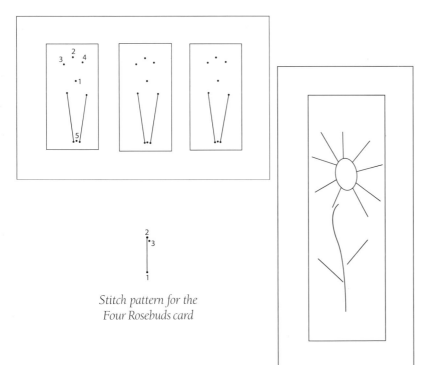

· base of stem   bud

2
3 ·
· 1

Stitch pattern for the
Four Rosebuds card

These templates for the cards shown opposite are all printed half
size, so you will need to enlarge them 100% on a photocopier.

Clockwise from top left:

Violas

These tiny pansies are centre ribbon stitches worked in 7mm (¼in) ribbon. Work the two top petals first, then the lower three. Use a second needle as in step 11 to create the round petal shape. Using 4mm (⅛in) pale yellow ribbon, work a small straight stitch over the lower three petals and deep yellow to work a two-loop French knot into each centre.

Rosebud Fan

Pale green fabric is set into card cut into a fan shape with a green thread to divide the panels. Buds are centre ribbon stitches worked in 7mm (¼in) ribbon, and then mounted on to the card blank.

A Single Sunflower

The petals are ribbon stitches worked in two shades of 4mm (⅛in) ribbon. Using deep gold (55) work the petals round in order as indicated, then fasten off. Continue to work round, using gold (54) to work petals between those already worked. Using a thread each of sand, brown and black stranded cotton together, work two-loop French knots to fill the centre. Work a straight stitch stem with six strands of sand embroidery thread and a single thread to couch and curve it in position. Add two 7mm (¼in) green ribbon stitch leaves to complete.

Four Rosebuds

The buds are worked on a piece of black linen on the straight of the grain, then cut to size and the the edges fringed. Using 7mm (¼in) ribbon, work a centre ribbon stitch and then a right ribbon stitch directly over the top. See step 19 to work the calyx in 2mm (¹⁄₁₆in) green ribbon.

A Trio of Tulips

The tulips are worked with 7mm (¼in) ribbon in yellow (15), orange (40) and red (02). Refer to steps 1–13 and 15 to prepare the card and embroider the flowers and stems. Anchor a length of green 7mm (¼in) ribbon at the base of a stem and work a ribbon stitch leaf. Fasten off. Work each leaf in turn. I have glued a coloured card behind the embroidered card to highlight it.

Tip

Stitch petals in order round a centre.
Never take the ribbon across the centre
of a flower at the back, as it will cause
problems when stitching through it.

Fuchsias

Silk ribbon gathered with a row of tiny running stitches is used to create a completely different range of flowers. The flowers will vary depending on the width of ribbon used, the length gathered and of course the colour. These fuchsias are delightful and by using a little paint, you can transform them.

You will need

Single-fold white card blank,
10.5 x 15cm (4¹⁄₈ x 6in)

White card, 8.5 x 12cm
(3¼ x 4¾in)

White fabric,
8cm (3¹⁄₈in) square

Glass-headed pin, mapping pin
and foam mat

Craft knife and cutting mat

Glue stick

Silk paints: red, magenta
and yellow

Paintbrushes, tile,
kitchen sponge and an iron

Needles: a size 13 (extra large)
and two size 18 (medium)
chenille and a crewel size 8

13mm (½in) silk ribbon:
50cm (20in) of pale pink (05)

7mm (¼in) silk ribbon:
50cm (20in) of dusky red (114)
25cm (10in) of deep green (21)

4mm (¹⁄₈in) silk ribbon:
50cm (20in) of dusky red (114)
25cm (10in) of deep green (21)

Toning stranded
embroidery thread and green
coton à broder

Scissors and tweezers

Clear silicone sealant

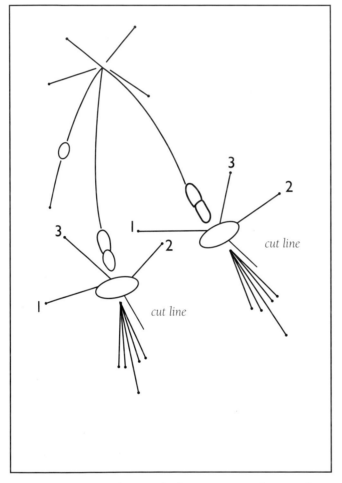

The pattern for the Fuchsias card. Photocopy it to make a template.

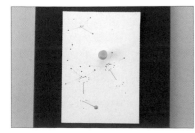

1. Use the template, a glass-headed pin, a mapping pin and a foam mat to transfer the design on to the piece of white card.

Tip
Gathered flowers are worked using short lengths of ribbon – a perfect way to use up your odds and ends. Always use a toning thread to gather ribbon.

2. Use the craft knife to cut round the oval shapes where the flower petals will sit.

3. Use a glue stick to stick the white fabric on the back of the card.

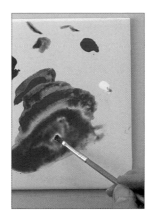

4. Mix the red, magenta and yellow silk paints on the tile to create the colour for the fuchsia.

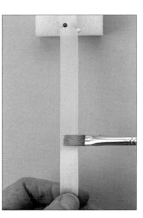

5. Pin one end of the 13mm (½in) pale pink ribbon to the kitchen sponge, then use a paintbrush to wet the ribbon.

6. Use a small brush to apply colour to one side of the ribbon. Note how it spreads across the ribbon.

7. Add more colour down the selvedge of the ribbon and hang it up to dry. Iron the ribbon to set the silk paint.

Tip

Silk dries very quickly, but if you wish to speed up the process, a hairdryer is useful. It will also stop paint from spreading too far if too much has been used on either ribbon or fabric.

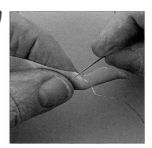

8. Knot the end of a strand of toning thread and take it through one end of the painted ribbon, 1cm (³/₈in) from the tail end, on the pale edge. Make a stitch over the edge to anchor the thread to the selvedge.

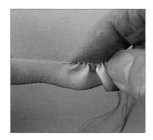

9. Start to work tiny running stitches along the selvedge.

10. Work a 10cm (4in) length of running stitch, then trim the ribbon diagonally 1cm (³/₈in) from the last stitch. Do not cut the thread.

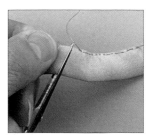

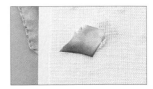

11. Use a craft knife and cutting mat to cut a slot through the card and fabric below each oval.

12. Use the flat end of a pair of tweezers to push the knotted end of the ribbon through the slot in the right-hand flower, with the stitched edge nearest the centre.

13. On the back of the panel, adjust the angle of the ribbon in the slot so that it is parallel to the cut end. Secure the tail with glue.

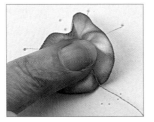

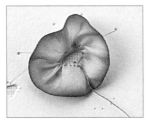

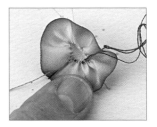

14. Pull the running stitch thread slightly to start the gather, then repeat steps 12 and 13 to secure the other end of the ribbon. The running stitch thread must stay on top.

15. Place a finger in the centre of the loop of ribbon, then gently pull the running stitch to gather the selvedge.

16. Keep checking the size of the gathered loop until it fits the edge of the cutout oval shape.

17. Using a toning thread, work in stab stitch along the gathered edge from the knotted end around to the right-hand end of the oval, tight to the card.

18. Fold the top of the gathered ribbon down, then stab stitch the selvedge, tight to the card, across the top of the oval.

19. Open up the gathered ribbon and stab stitch the left-hand side of the bottom of the oval. Take the working thread and the gathering stitch thread to the back of the panel and tie off both.

20. Using 7mm (¼in) dusky red ribbon, work a loose ribbon stitch over the frill, taking the needle down through the top edge of the ribbon at 1. Repeat for petal 2 and work a centre ribbon stitch at 3. Then use 4mm (⅛in) ribbon the same colour to work the straight stitch tube. Add a tiny 4mm (⅛in) deep green stitch at the top. Use pink and white embroidery thread to work straight stitches with French knots (see page 38) at the ends to form the stamens.

21. Work the second flower in the same way, then add a straight stitch bud. The stems are coton à broder straight stitches and the leaves are ribbon stitch using 7mm (¼in) deep green ribbon.

The finished card

I attached the panel to the folded card blank using clear silicone sealant as described on page 110. When it was dry, I used a 4mm (⅛in) dusky red ribbon to highlight the design, using the following method. Use a mapping pin to make holes in three corners of the card front and in the bow position as shown. Tie a small looped bow in the centre of the ribbon and pull the knot tight. Leaving a long end at the back, anchor the bow in position with a stitch in a toning thread, then use this thread to work a stitch to anchor the ribbon at the corner. Now tie off the ends to secure them. Keep the ribbon flat on the front and, referring to page 107 steps 6 and 7, anchor the ends on the back of the card.

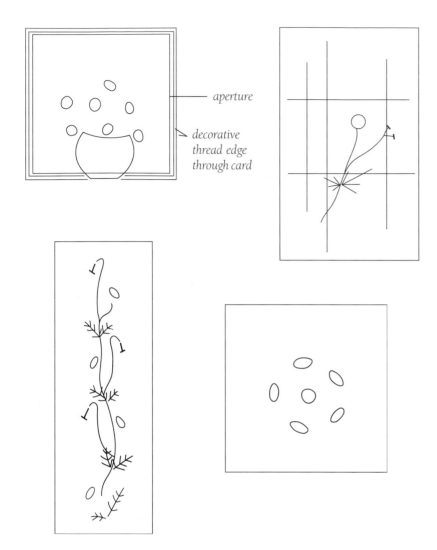

aperture

decorative
thread edge
through card

*These templates for the cards shown opposite are all printed
half size, so you will need to enlarge them 100% on a
photocopier. You will not need a template for the left-hand
panel of the Scabious Garland card.*

Clockwise from bottom left:

Poppies

*Using red (02) 7mm (¼in) ribbon, gather
four 6cm (2¼in) lengths, plus a 1cm (³⁄₈in)
tail at each end. Now proceed as in steps
8–16, but use a chenille size 18 needle to
take the ribbon through the card. Gather the
ribbon evenly round the aperture, stab stitch
it in place and using two black threads, fill
the centres with two-loop French knots. Work
straight stitch buds with 7mm (¼in) moss
green (20) ribbon and add a straight stitch
stem, couching through the card with a
toning thread to curve it. Use this thread to
work the fly stitch leaves.*

Bowl of Anemones

*Glue pale green fabric in the aperture and
cut out the bowl shape. See page 37 steps 7
and 8 to shape and position. Work the flowers
as for the poppies using 7mm (¼in) ribbon in
deep pink (128), delph blue (117), deep red
(49) and purple (177), then work two-loop
French knots in black to fill the centres.
Using green coton à broder, work tiny fan
shapes for the leaves. Edge the card with two-
coloured threads.*

Buttercup

*Cut a piece of black linen on the straight of
the grain, fringe each side and press. Make
holes for flowers in a piece of card and stick it
behind the fabric but not the fringe, and
make holes for flowers. Work the flower and
bud (two stitches) as for the poppies with
7mm (¼in) yellow (15) ribbon, then the
stamens as for the clematis centres on page
22. Couch the two thread lines in position
and work the two straight stitches with 2mm
(¹⁄₁₆in) moss green ribbon. Work the stem and
add leaves using 2mm (¹⁄₁₆in) green ribbon.*

Scabious Garland

*Prepare both white panels as in steps 2 and
3. Mix blue silk paint with a hint of magenta
to shade 66cm (26in) of 7mm (¼in) white
(03) ribbon patchily. Dry then press the
ribbon. Work as for the poppies but gather
seven 6cm (2¼in) lengths plus 1cm (³⁄₈in)
tails and use a strand each of pale green and
yellow for the centres. Work the stem and
leaves as for the garland on page 21.*

Tip
To make an edging as in the Bowl of Anemones card: make a pinhole at each
corner of the card, thread a needle with a coloured thread and take it down through
a hole, leaving half of the thread at the front. Lay the top thread over the next hole
and bring the needle up, over and back down to hold this thread. Keeping the top
thread taut, work the next two corners, unthread the needle and use it to take the
top thread down at the start. Tie the ends off securely. Repeat with a second colour.

Beaded Cards

by Patricia Wing

There are so many techniques you can use for cardmaking, and using beads, gems and lace with pricking and embossing techniques will considerably add to your repertoire.

There is a wealth of templates available for pricking out and stencils for embossing, to help create that extra special card. Most templates and stencils are a pleasure to work with, as someone has already created the design – you only have to follow the pattern, so pricking out or embossing could not be easier.

Stitching on beads adds another dimension, as do all the lovely gems. Beautiful lace will also complement the beadwork and you will be surprised at the originality you can achieve by cutting out designs from within the lace.

Although your cards will take longer to complete if you add these techniques, you will feel that the finished work is well worth all the effort. You can, of course, design your own beaded cards but pricking out the design first really helps with stitching on the beads.

The Victorians produced some extraordinarily beautiful cards, which form an important part of the heritage they bequeathed to us. Equally, the cards you create could become future family heirlooms that your family will cherish in years to come.

Keep an eye open for inexpensive jewellery – old earrings and brooches often have attractive glass gems that will enhance your work and make it unique. You can find all sorts of things in charity shops, and locally I visit an auction house where boxes of broken jewellery and oddments can yield a treasure-trove of embellishments for my cards!

Pat Wing

Opposite
These cards show some of the effects that can be created using beads, gems, pricking and embossing techniques and lace in your card making.

Materials

Templates and stencils

There is now huge range of templates for pricking and stencils for embossing available, which give you professionally designed patterns to use. The fun comes from selecting which parts of these designs you want to use to create your own unique work. Most embossing stencils are made from unpainted brass, whilst pricking templates are usually metal with a painted finish.

Envelope and tag templates are also very useful. They are made from flexible plastic and are transparent so that you can see where you are placing them on your card.

Pricking templates and embossing stencils shown with envelope and tag templates.

Tools

A cutting mat is a must, and those printed with a fine grid can be a great help when squaring or measuring card and paper. A craft knife and metal ruler are used for cutting card. Fancy-edged scissors are used to add decorative edges, as are corner scissors.

It goes without saying that your HB pencil must be kept sharp at all times for accurate work, so keep a sharpener to hand as well as an eraser.

Three sizes of embossing tool are sufficient to fit most stencils. When choosing a light box for embossing, go for one at least 20 x 30cm (8 x 12in), as this allows plenty of room to fix a stencil with tape and to rest your hand when working.

A pricking tool and pricking mat are used for pricking out designs.

A cocktail stick is used for picking up small gems.

Quilting needles in size 12 are most useful for stitching beads on to cards.

Use fine scissors for cutting out lace patterns and a pigment inkpad and dauber for dyeing them to your chosen colour. Kitchen paper is a must for keeping your work surface clean when colouring lace.

Craft punches are useful for punching out shapes to decorate your beaded cards. A single hole punch is used when adding tassels or ribbons to bookmarks or tags.

A metal ruler, pencil, eraser and sharpener, a light box, craft punches, a single hole punch, fancy-edged and corner scissors, a craft knife, needles, fine scissors, a cocktail stick, pricking and embossing tools, a pricking mat, pigment inkpad, dauber and kitchen paper, all on a cutting mat.

Sticky things

Low tack masking tape is used to stick your stencils or templates to the light box or to card, as it can easily be removed. Double-sided tape is very useful for layering card and the finger lift variety is especially easy to use. Small 3D foam squares are ideal for giving a three-dimensional aspect to your work. A fine-tipped PVA glue applicator is useful for sticking small gems to your work.

Cards and papers

I often used ready-made card blanks and cut them down to the size required, which can be a real time-saver. You can of course always make up your own cards – the material needs to be quite firm especially if you are pricking out and stitching.

Pastel paper is ideal for embossing and stitching but as it is only 160gsm (90lb), it needs to be applied to a firmer card so that it will stand up.

Parchment is an extremely versatile material as it can be used for embossing and stitching, it will readily accept colour, it can be made into flowers or used as inserts and it comes in a huge range of colours.

Card, pastel paper and parchment in a range of colours.

124

Beads, lace and other embellishments

There is such an array of beautiful coloured beads that come in all shapes and sizes. It is a pleasure to work with beads: they really do enhance one's cards. You can stitch them or glue them on.

There is also a stunning collection of cabouchons: flat-backed gems. They are made from glass or acrylic and are faceted or smooth. Imitation cameos also work well with beads. Imitation pearls come in an assortment of colours and shapes, also flat-backed.

Just studying the various intricate designs worked in lace will inspire you. Bridal motifs along with your beads and gems make stunning wedding cards.

There is an abundance of coloured threads which have many applications – stitching decorative borders is just one. Silk ribbons can be worked into the designs not only for cards but also for bookmarks and gift tags.

Beads, gems, imitation pearls, silk ribbon,
thread, an imitation cameo and lace,
all used to decorate cards.

Basic techniques

The techniques used to make the cards in this book, such as embossing and pricking, are easy to learn and perfect for beginners. You will be amazed at the beautiful cards you can make with a few simple techniques.

Punching shapes

Craft punches are a fantastic asset to card making – you just punch out the pattern, which could not be easier. Often you can choose to layer the shapes as punch patterns come in several different sizes.

1. Place the paper in the punch.

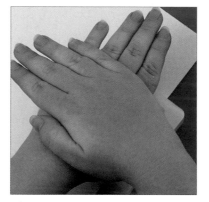

2. Press down firmly to cut through the paper.

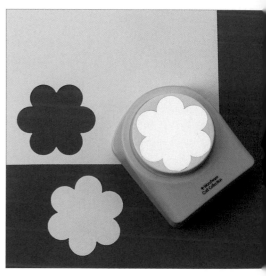

3. The punched paper falls out underneath the punch.

Craft punches come in all shapes and sizes, and as shown here you can often punch the same shape in several sizes.

Pricking out

When pricking out to give a decorative pattern, the finished design can have a flat or a raised finish. These are achieved by pricking through your card either from the front (flat) or the reverse (raised).

1. Tape the template to the back of the card using masking tape. Pricking from the back creates a raised effect.

2. On a mat, use a pricking tool to prick through the holes in the template.

3. Peel off the tape and turn the card over to reveal the pattern.

The same design pricked from the front gives a flatter, softer effect.

Gluing on beads or gems

A fine-tipped PVA glue applicator makes it very easy to apply the smaller gems to your work – there is nothing worse than surplus glue!

1. Use a fine-tipped PVA glue applicator to place dots of glue where required.

2. Use a cocktail stick with a tiny bit of glue on the end to pick up a gem and place it on a glue dot on the design.

3. Press the gem with the other end of the cocktail stick to secure it.

The finished design.

Embossing with a light box

Embossing is done from the back of the card with a rounded tool which pushes the card into the pattern of the stencil. This gives an elegant, raised finish on the front of the card.

1. Using masking tape, fix the stencil to the centre of the light box. Switch on the light.

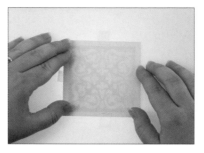

2. Tape the card over the stencil, right side down.

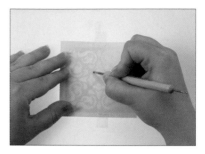

3. Press the embossing tool into the pattern as required.

4. You can select all or only part of the stencil pattern to suit your card design. When it is finished, peel off the tape and turn the card over to see the design.

Sewing on beads

This technique requires the template to be taped to the face of the card to give a flat finish, and you only need to prick through very lightly as a guide for the beading needle. It is best to use thread close in colour to the background of the card.

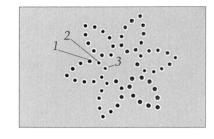

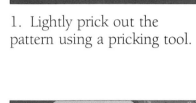

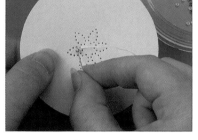

1. Lightly prick out the pattern using a pricking tool.

2. Tape the end of the thread to the back of the card.

3. Bring the thread through hole 2 and pick up a bead on your needle.

4. Secure the bead by going down hole 1.

5. Bring the needle up in hole 3 and pick up another bead.

6. Go down in hole 2.

7. Move on to the next group of three holes and continue in the same way to finish the design. Secure the end of the thread at the back with tape as you did at the start.

Folding card

You may want to make your own cards. A cutting mat can be used to centre the fold of your card, or you can measure and mark the card. Whichever way you choose, accuracy is very important.

1. Mark the centre of the card with a pencil on the top and bottom edge, using the grid on your cutting mat as a guide.

2. Line up the ruler with the marks and score the card with a small embossing tool.

3. Fold along the scored line.

Making a border

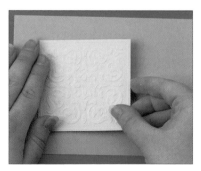

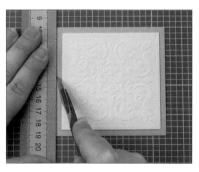

1. To make a fine border, stick the design on to to a larger piece of coloured paper using double-sided tape.

2. Use the grid on your cutting mat to measure the width of the border, and trim the paper using a ruler and craft knife.

3. Cut the other three sides to the same width, using the grid as a guide.

Tip
Take your time when trimming to ensure a neat cut.

Making gem flowers

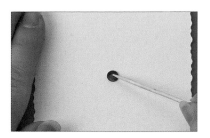

1. Glue the gem for the flower centre on to paper, as shown on page 127.

2. Use a fine-tipped PVA glue applicator to place a circle of glue around the gem.

3. Use a cocktail stick to place oval pearls around the gem, pressing down towards the centre of the flower.

4. When the glue is dry, trim the paper away.

Dyeing lace

This technique allows you to colour pieces of lace the exact shade you need to match or complement your other embellishments. Here I use a pigment inkpad and a dauber.

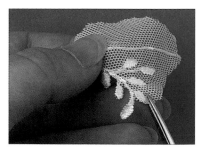

1. Cut out the part of the lace using fine scissors.

2. Place it on kitchen paper to keep your work surface clean. Tap the dauber on to the pigment ink pad.

3. Transfer the colour to the lace by tapping with the dauber. Leave to dry.

The finished dyed lace.

Pearl Daisies

A good starter card using pricking and gem gluing techniques. A basic lightly textured ivory card blank is decorated with pearl droplets and lilac gems and set off with a lilac paper border. The design can be varied by using different colour schemes.

You will need

Ivory card blank, folded size 123 x 152mm (4^7/$_8$ x 6in)

Insert paper, 80gsm (20lb) same size

Pricking tool and mat

Pricking template PRO555

Lilac paper, 118 x 148mm (4^5/$_8$ x 5^7/$_8$in)

Cream card, 110 x 80mm (4^3/$_8$ x 3^1/$_8$in)

Sixteen lilac gems, 3mm (^{1}/$_8$in)

Four lilac faceted gems, 5mm (^{3}/$_{16}$in)

Twenty white oval pearls

Twenty lilac oval pearls

Fine-tipped PVA glue applicator and cocktail stick

Craft knife and cutting mat

Double-sided tape

Masking tape

1. Place the template on the back of the card so that the motif is in the corner. Tape it down.

2. Place the card on a pricking mat and prick through the holes.

3. Move the template to the next corner and repeat.

4. Continue with the other two corners.

5. Take the piece of cream card, line up the motif on the stencil at the top of the card and tape it down.

6. Prick the pattern, then move the template to the bottom of the card and repeat.

7. Line up the motif at the side of the card, and prick again. Repeat the other side.

8. Stick the pricked cream card on to the lilac paper using double-sided tape.

9. Trim the paper to leave a 5mm (³/₁₆in) border, using a craft knife and cutting mat.

10. Stick the lilac paper to the centre of the main pricked card blank using double-sided tape.

11. Make two white and two lilic daisies using the technique shown on page 131.

12. Stick the daisies in place as shown using PVA glue.

13. Use a fine-tipped PVA glue applicator to make dots of glue where the gems will go. Pick up gems using a cocktail stick with a little glue on the end and stick them in place.

Tip

For a professional
finish, always make an
insert for your card.

14. Fold the insert paper in half.

15. Open the card and stick the insert to the spine using dots of PVA
glue from the applicator.

Opposite

*The finished card. The
pearl daisies set off the
swirling pricked design
perfectly and the purple
gems and border make
this a subtle yet striking
card for any occasion.*

Top: Two flowers were punched out and stuck to the centre as shown. I used pricking template PR0559 for pricking out the central circle, and embossed the circle containing the ring of amber beads using the same template. Bottom: The large green daisy sits on a scalloped punched shape. I wound gold thread round it and then used a 3D foam square to stick the shape on to a circle of green leaf parchment. The corners of the square card were embossed using stencil EF8004. The pricked out design comes from template PRO536. The embellishments are flat-backed gems.

Top: The white art deco wallet was made up using white marbled card. The technique shown on page 15 was used to make the daisy. I used pricking template PRO536 for the corners. Art Deco corner scissors give the decorative stepped effect. Bottom: stencil 5801S was used in various ways to create this card. Each corner of the card blank was embossed first, then the centre panel of the card, and finally the edge of the stencil was used to emboss the square shape, which was then mounted on to gold card.

Lilac and Lace

Lilac stitched beads and parchment blend together so well to complement a selected piece of white lace. The corners of the lightly textured card are embossed to add further elegance.

You will need
Light box
Cream card blank, folded size
120mm x 175mm
(4¾ x 6⁷/₈in)
A5 cream card
Stencils 5802S and EF8013
Template PR0507
Masking tape
Lilac seed beads
Lilac parchment
Pricking tool and mat
Embossing tool
Pencil
Fine scissors
Piece of lace
Fine-tipped PVA glue
applicator
Double-sided tape

1. Tape the embossing stencil on the light box.

2. Open the card blank and tape it in place as shown. Emboss the corner using the embossing tool. Emboss each of the other three corners in the same way.

The card with the four corners embossed.

3. Tape the stencil on the front of the card with the pricking out design in the corner, just inside the embossed design. Prick out the design in each corner, using a pricking tool and mat.

4. Sew on the beads as shown on page 13.

5. Using the same pricking out design on purple parchment, prick out the pattern four times.

6. Using the prick marks as a guide, cut out teardrop shapes from the parchment.

7. Using your scissors to pick up the teardrop shapes, place them inside the beaded shapes.

8. Apply masking tape to the parts of the oval template that will not be used.

9. Stick the stencil on to lilac parchment. Turn the parchment over and run the medium embossing tool around the top half of the template.

10. Realign the template ready to do the bottom half.

 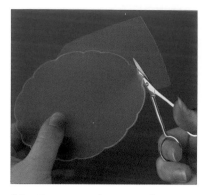 

11. Run the embossing tool around the bottom half.

12. Remove the template and cut around the outside of the embossed line.

13. Stick the stencil to the A5 cream card and pencil round the top edge.

14. Prick the last hole on each side as shown.

15. Realign the template using the pricked holes as a guide and pencil around the bottom edge.

16. Cut out the shape.

18. Stitch on lilac beads around the border as shown on page 13.

17. Reapply the template and lightly prick the edge.

142

19. Cut out the lace motif.

20. Mount the lace on to lilac parchment using dots of glue behind heavy areas of lace. Trim away the edges.

21. Mount the lace and parchment on to the beaded cream card using double-sided tape.

22. Mount these on to the lilac parchment oval in the same way.

23. Mount the artwork on to the main card.

The finished card. Keeping to a simple colour scheme enhances this card, and putting the lace over the lilac parchment coordinates the overall design.

Top left: Use part of template PR0505 to prick out the basic pattern for stitching, then use the flower design in the corner of the template to make the two flowers in the centre of the card. Stitch the outline in pale turquoise and ivory beads before gluing the appropriate beads into the patterns. Cut out and stick on pale turquoise lace before adding the final bead embellishments.

Top right: Using template PR0554 for the centre and PR0559 for the corners, I have pricked out the simple but effective design you see stitched with pale yellow seed beads. Twelve large, pale, amber flat-backed teardrops are glued on and cut-out lace is repeated in the four corners. The central lace flower has been enhanced with tiny pale yellow beads.

Bottom left: Template PR0558 is used to prick out raised patterns at the sides and a flat pattern for stitching on beads in the centre. Two strips of white lace backed with pink parchment are then laid between the patterns.

Bottom right: The square card has embossed corners from stencil 5802S. The design is pricked out from template PR0536 after first embossing the edge of the template in to the card. Pale amber seed beads are stitched on, flat-backed pearls are added and the white seed beads are glued into the amber patterns. The lace is added last.

Three-dimensional Cards

by Dawn Allen

Cutting paper to create three-dimensional images started in the nineteenth century, when two identical images were placed on top of each other and separated by a mixture of paste and straw. In the mid- to late twentieth century this was developed into a three-dimensional art form by cutting pieces from several identical prints and layering the cut pieces on to a base image. The spaces between the layers were created using spots of silicone sealant.

Three-dimensional paper decoration has become very popular in recent years with the growing interest in hand-produced cards. Handmade cards are ideal for any occasion, and make a person feel extra special because you have taken the time and trouble to create a beautiful card just for them. In addition, you will have gained a great deal of pleasure from making it! A finished card can, of course, be framed as a permanent keepsake.

Three-dimensional greetings cards can be made from almost any paper image, such as prints, wrapping paper, or designs you have created yourself. You can use as few as four identical images to make a three-dimensional picture, and as many as twenty or thirty can be used to create a truly magnificent sculptured artwork. In general, the more images you use, the more detailed will be the finished picture. Finally, coating the image with a paper glaze will produce an exquisite porcelain effect which not only enhances the colours but also protects your work.

Three-dimensional cards are stronger than they look, though they should be protected with a piece of bubble wrap before posting, or you can use a padded envelope or card box if you prefer.

I wish you every success and enjoyment with your cardmaking, and always remember that you will never make a mistake – it may be 'just a little bit different', that's all!

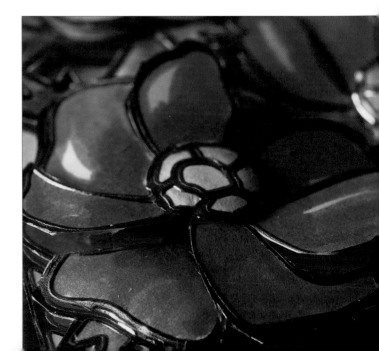

Middle left, bottom right ©2005 Morehead, Inc; top left ©2005 Reina, N.Y.

A selection of greetings cards that have been made using the techniques described in this book.

Materials

Cards and papers

It is important that you choose the right card on which to mount your three-dimensional picture. If the colours or textures are not quite compatible with your image, the whole look of the card will be spoiled.

Card blanks can be bought in various sizes and colours, with or without apertures or decorative edges, or alternatively you can cut your own card to size from individual sheets, using a rotary paper trimmer. Trimmers are available that allow you to produce your own decorative edges simply by changing the blades. Alternatively you can cut the card to size using a metal ruler and a craft knife.

A gorgeous array of decorative papers and cards is available to use for card inserts, matching envelopes and backing panels (mat mounts). They can also be used to cover the facing page of the inside of a card. Papers come in numerous weights, textures and designs. There are some superb handmade papers, for example mulberry papers, which are made from pulped mulberry leaves. These are very versatile and can be cut and frayed to give a spectacular effect.

Printed sheets and stamps

You can make a beautiful three-dimensional card from any number of prints, ones you have either created yourself or taken from a pre-printed sheet designed especially for three-dimensional paper crafts. These sheets have four or more identical images on them from which you can select the parts of the finished picture you want to build up to create a three-dimensional effect. Alternatively, you can use one of the numerous step-by-step sheets that you can buy, on which the layered parts of the picture are numbered in the order in which they are to be used.

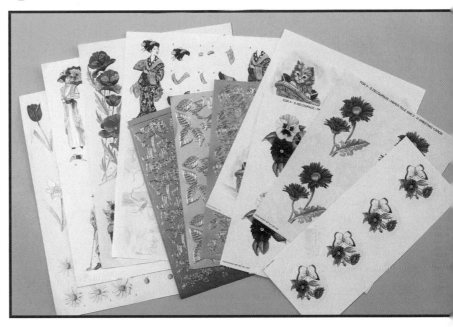

You can also create designs using outline craft stickers, which come in a range of finishes and colours, or stamped images. I like using watercolour pens to add colour because they are so easy to use and you can produce gorgeous effects by blending colours together and adding water to make them lighter, but the type of paint, pen or crayon you use is really down to personal choice. Experiment with different media and see what amazing finishes you can produce!

If you decide to invest in a set of watercolour pens, it is also worth purchasing a blender pen. Mix colours on a sheet of acetate, then use the blender pen to pick up the colours and apply them to your picture. This gives a softer effect than applying the pens directly to the card.

If you are using rubber stamps, make sure you use a solvent-based inkpad as this type of ink will not bleed when you apply colour to the image, and for the best results stamp on to medium-weight card. This weight of card works well with moulded or shaped cut pieces.

Embellishments

There is such a good range of paper embellishments available today that you can really let your imagination run wild! Add stick-on ribbons, multicoloured feathers, decorative papers, glitter, sequins and tiny beads to make your card extra special. Use craft stickers to decorate your card or to add a simple greeting such as 'happy birthday' or 'good luck'.

Take care when choosing which embellishments to add to a card – they should be used to enhance the design and not detract from it. Use colours, styles and textures that work together to create a coherent look, and do not fall into the trap of over-decorating your card. Use embellishments sparingly and thoughtfully, and don't be afraid to add no extra decoration at all if the card works well without it.

Other equipment

To cut out your images, you will need either a small pair of **sharp-pointed scissors**, or a **craft knife** that can take a standard size 10A blade. Always make sure you have a good supply of **spare blades**. A **steel ruler** is useful for achieving straight edges. The best surface for cutting on is a self-healing **cutting mat**, which 'heals itself' after a fine cut (see page 152). For rubber stamping, a **stamping mat** is also very useful, though not essential.

For shaping your cut-out pieces you will need a round-ended, a pointed, a flat-ended and a spoon-shaped **wooden shaping tool**. Use them in conjunction with a **pencil eraser** for hard shaping, or a **foam pad** (the sort used for applying make-up) for soft shaping (see page 155).

For attaching the various layers of the image, I use either **silicone sealant** or **3D foam squares**. Silicone sealant sets hard and can be applied as raised spots of glue to create depth between the layers. 3D foam squares have the same effect but are less flexible (see page 156).

Tweezers, both long and angled, are useful for manipulating small cut-out pieces and for manoeuvring them into position. **Cocktail sticks** can also be used to position cut-out pieces, and to apply the silcone sealant.

If you wish to glaze your image, you will need a **paintbrush** and **brush cleaner**.

Fancy-edged scissors are useful for adding a decorative edge to your card or backing paper. **Rotary paper trimmers** achieve very much the same result as scissors, and come with different patterned **cutting wheels**. Alternatively, a **paper guillotine** allows you to produce perfectly straight edges.

Use either **double-sided tape** or **adhesive dots** (available on a continuous roll in a refillable dispenser) to attach pieces of decorative card or paper to your greetings card, and to attach your finished three-dimensional image. Adhesive dots are especially useful as they are available in both repositionable and permanent form.

Finally, if you decide to decorate your cards using **eyelets**, a **mechanical eyelet tool** is an excellent way of fixing them in place.

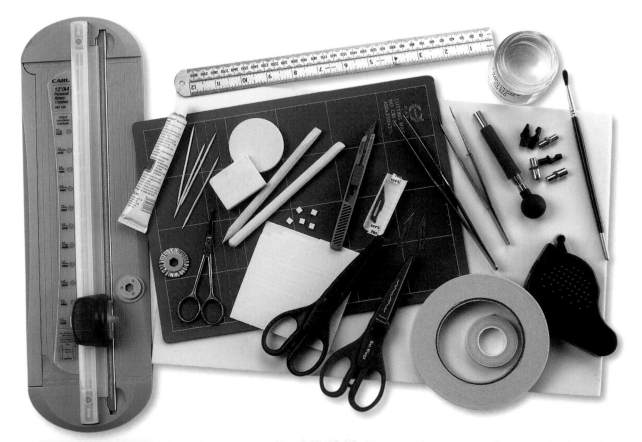

Basic techniques

There are several different methods of making three-dimensional cards. I am going to explain how to use pre-printed sheets, step-by-step sheets, outline craft stickers and rubber stamps. All the materials used in these projects can be obtained through good craft outlets.

Before starting on the projects it is a good idea to practise the basic techniques used in cutting, shaping and mounting.

Cutting using a craft knife

There are two methods of cutting: using either a pair of sharp-pointed scissors or a craft knife. It can be difficult to cut fine, intricate shapes with scissors, whereas if you learn to cut correctly with a craft knife you can achieve much greater precision, and the finished product looks far better. You will need a knife that is capable of taking a standard size 10A blade, which is flexible and which has a very sharp cutting point.

The basic technique for cutting using a craft knife is very simple. If you pick up a pencil and start to write or draw, you will notice that you are holding the pencil at a slight angle –hold your knife in exactly the same way.

You will need a board to cut on. Do not use a chopping board, bread board or anything with a hard surface as this will only blunt the blade and leave raised edges under your work which will make cutting difficult. The best surface is a self-healing cutting mat which, as the name implies, seals itself after a fine cut and therefore retains a smooth, flat surface.

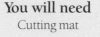
You will need
Cutting mat
Craft knife that holds a
size 10A blade

Tip
Always use a sharp blade
in your craft knife – a
blunt one may tear the
paper. You will achieve far
better results if you
always start a project
with a new blade.

1. When you begin cutting, relax, hold the knife comfortably at an angle of about 30° to the cutting surface and cut gently in a flowing movement around the outline of the shape. In this way you are effectively bevelling the paper by cutting away the underneath part so that the white edge of the paper will not be visible.

2. Start at the top and work down the right-hand side of the piece to be cut. Turn the paper as you cut, following the outline.

3. Keep the knife on the right-hand side of the cut so the cutting line is always visible. There is no need to press too hard.

Tip
Reverse Step 3 if you are left-handed.

Furring and feathering

You can use either a craft knife or scissors to create the effect of fur or feathers, though a knife will always give you a finer finish – you do not want your animal to end up looking as though it needs grooming!

To achieve this effect successfully, the angle of your knife or scissors is important.

1. Angle the knife from side to side, making a criss-cross pattern.

2. Lengthen and shorten the cuts as necessary to obtain a fur-like effect.

Tip

With this technique it is sometimes necessary to colour in the edge. Do this using watercolour pens/pencils. Always use a shade lighter than the actual image, and colour from the back to hide any white edges.

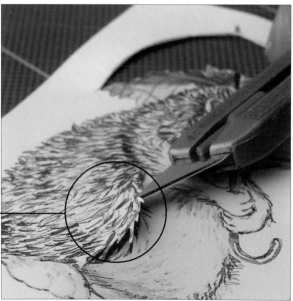

3. The closer you make the cuts, the finer the furring/feathering will be.

Shaping

Shaping is an essential part of three-dimensional picture sculpture. To achieve natural-looking shapes you need to visualise the subject in real life and then re-create it in three dimensions. Use wooden shaping tools in conjunction with a small foam pad or an eraser to avoid creasing or tearing the piece you are shaping.

Only the top pieces of the image (the pieces that are not covered by another piece) need to be shaped. To achieve the required shape, place the cut piece face down on either an eraser or a foam pad and gently roll it into the required shape using the shaped end of a shaping tool.

Be gentle and keep the shaping slight; if you over-shape the piece it will not fit completely over the piece behind it. When you have achieved the desired result, hold the piece in position with tweezers to see if the shape is correct. If it is, then apply; if not then re-shape it and try again.

You will need
Wooden shaping tools
Pencil eraser
Foam pad

For a firm, rounded shape such as leaves or berries, apply hard shaping using a pencil eraser and a pointed shaping tool.

For softer curves, apply soft shaping using a foam pad and a rounded shaping tool.

Mounting

There are two methods of mounting the pieces: using either 3D foam squares or silicone sealant.

Sealant will give a better result, as you can control the height and width of the sealant by applying it to your work using a cocktail stick. Use approximately 3–5mm (¼in) of silicone between the base print and the first layer, and approximately 2–3mm (⅛in) between subsequent layers. If you can, leave the first layer to dry for five to ten minutes. By leaving this piece to cure it makes it easier to apply the rest of the pieces.

You will need
Silicone sealant
3mm (⅛in) 3D foam squares
Cocktail sticks for applying the silicone sealant
Angled and straight tweezers
Craft knife

If you are using 3D foam squares, apply a square to the back of the piece, and gently lift off the backing using the tip of a craft knife.

Tip
If you are using 3D foam squares, put two squares together to obtain extra height.

Once you have applied either silicone sealant or foam squares to your cut-out piece, use tweezers to place the piece on your image and if necessary use a clean cocktail stick for fine adjustments. If you have used silicone sealant, do not use your fingers to push the piece down on to the work as it will flatten and spread the glue over the edges; use a cocktail stick.

If you are using silicone sealant, transfer the required amount of sealant on to a cocktail stick.

Apply it to your work using a rolling motion.

Tip
Keep the silicone away from the edges of the print to avoid it being seen on the finished card.

Glazing

Glazing can certainly enhance a card by creating a porcelain effect, but it is really a matter of personal preference. It is not always necessary to glaze the whole card; select the parts that you feel would be accentuated by glazing. Remember always to test a scrap piece of your work first to make sure it is colourfast.

It is necessary to apply only a single coat of glaze. Allow three to four hours for the glaze to dry, and remember to clean your brush immediately after use using a spirit-based brush cleaner.

You will need

High-gloss paper glaze
Camel hair paintbrush
Spirit-based brush cleaner

1. Load the paintbrush with glaze, transfer it to the image and allow the glaze to drop on to the image from a height of about 0.5cm (¼in).

2. Pull the glaze down the image with the brush. Repeat until the glazing is complete.

Caution

To use high-gloss paper glaze safely, use it only in a well-ventilated area, avoid breathing in the fumes directly, and keep the glaze well away from naked flames. Children must not be allowed to use paper glaze unsupervised.

The finished glazed flower.

Oriental Beauty

For this card I used a step-by-step sheet. These sheets are an excellent introduction to three-dimensional paper craft, as you simply need to cut round the numbered pieces and mount them in numerical order. It is best to cut out everything first before attempting to assemble the card.

Oriental designs have always been popular, and this card's bold, joyful colours coupled with the Japanese greeting of goodwill make it ideal for any celebration.

You will need

Step-by-step sheet
(Klein Design 127)

Red A5 card blank,
148 x 210mm (6 x 8¼in)

Blue card,
130 x 180mm (5 x 7in)

Japanese greeting craft sticker

Permanent adhesive dots or
double-sided tape

Silicone sealant

Tweezers, straight and angled

Cocktail sticks

3mm (⅛in) 3D foam squares

Craft knife and spare blades

Cutting mat

Fancy-edged scissors

Shaping tools

Eraser

Foam pad

Pencil

Steel ruler

1. Begin by cutting out the background scene using a steel ruler and a craft knife.

2. Cut out the complete figure using the technique described on pages 152–153. This is the base on which the three-dimensional image will be built up.

3. As you work around the figure, move the paper to achieve the correct position for cutting.

4. Cut out the remaining pieces. Make sure you keep them in the right order – pencil the number on the back of each piece. As with all step-by-step sheets, you will be attaching the cut-out shapes to the base figure in numerical order.

The complete set of cut-out pieces.

5. Shape the head of the base figure by placing it face down on an eraser and rubbing it firmly with the back of the spoon-shaped shaping tool.

6. Shape the skirt by resting it on the foam pad and gently rolling the shaping tool backwards and forwards over it.

7. Shape the cut-out hair using the same technique as you used for the head.

8. Apply silicone sealant to the back of the hair using a cocktail stick.

9. Pick up the cut-out hair using straight tweezers and position it over the hair on the base figure.

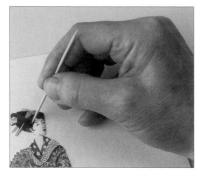

11. Apply silicone sealant to the next shape in the sequence (the hair comb). Because it is so small, you will find it easier to hold the shape using the tweezers.

10. Manoeuvre the cut-out hair into position using a cocktail stick.

12. Position the comb on the hair of the base figure. Position the second hair comb in the same way.

13. Gently shape the next piece in the sequence – the left-hand cuff – using the pointed shaping tool. Shape the edges only, leaving the middle part flat.

14. Glue the cuff into position on the base figure using silicone sealant.

  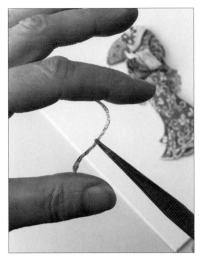

15. Shape the skirt of the cut-out dress in the same way as in Step 6. Apply a spot of silicone sealant to each end of the piece. Do not spread it out.

16. Apply the dress to the base figure. The two spots of silicone sealant raise the cut-out piece above the background, producing a three-dimensional effect. Allow fifteen minutes for the silicone sealant to dry before moving on to the next step.

17. Continue to shape and apply the cut-out pieces to the base figure. Shape the rim of the dress (shown in the photograph) by holding it in the tweezers and gently bending the ends downwards with your fingers. Apply a small spot of silicone sealant to each end, wipe away any excess with your fingers, and apply it to the base figure.

18. Now construct the flowers. Begin by shaping the base flower using hard shaping. Rest it on an eraser and rub it firmly with the spoon-shaped shaping tool.

19. Shape the next flower piece in the same way, apply a spot of silicone sealant to its centre and attach it to the base flower. Shape and apply the rest of the pieces.

The completed three-dimensional pictures. Leave them to dry completely before constructing the card. This should take approximately two hours.

20. To make the card, begin by giving a decorative edge to the card blank and the blue card, then attach the mat mount to the front of the greetings card. Attach the background scene to the mount, allowing enough room in the right-hand margin for the Japanese greeting.

Tip

To fix the mat mount into position, use double-sided tape or permanent adhesive dots.

21. Apply 3D foam squares to the back of the figure.

22. Attach the figure to the card. Complete the card by attaching the flower and the Japanese greeting craft sticker.

Oriental Beauty

I particularly like this card because of its sense of peace and tranquillity. The blue in the woman's dress is reflected in the blue mat mount and the peaceful background scene. This combination of red, blue and yellow is typical of oriental designs.

Snow Dance

This dainty little ballerina is mounted on a piece of thin purple paper with a delicately torn edge. The background has been decorated with tiny silver stick-on dots and rings which lend a magical, wintery feel to the design. A lovely card for a young girl with a Christmas birthday, perhaps.

These three cards have all been made using step-by-step sheets, and illustrate the range of designs available. Backing papers, cards and embellishments have been used to reinforce the cards' themes. In the bottom left-hand card, most of the three-dimensional picture is within the aperture, but some elements lie partly outside it. This is an effective way of giving added depth to a three-dimensional image.

A Gift for You

Using rubber stamps is a highly creative, versatile way to make three-dimensional cards. You can use the same stamp to make a wide variety of different cards simply by varying the colours and types of inks, pens and so on, and you can make as many images as you need. It is particularly satisfying if you enjoy colouring or painting. For this project I used watercolour pens, which give the same effect as watercolour paints but are easier to control.

You will need

Rubber stamp
(Fun Stamps F-M119 Gift Mouse)

Solvent-based inkpad

Medium-weight white A4 card

Stamping mat

Watercolour pens, blender and sheet of acetate for mixing colours

Cream A6 card blank,
105 x 148mm (4¼ x 6in), with 50mm (2in) square aperture

Pink card

Small red heart craft stickers

Permanent and repositionable adhesive dots or double-sided tape

Cutting mat

Craft knife and spare blades

Scissors

Silicone sealant

Cocktail sticks

Tweezers, straight and angled

Shaping tools

Foam pad

Eraser

1. Resting your work on a stamping mat, stamp five images on to the piece of white A4 card.

2. Using watercolour pens, apply colour to each of the images. Start with the lightest shades and end with the darkest. For the mouse's fur, apply the paint with a blender for a lighter, less solid appearance.

3. Cut out the shapes you need from your five images. Remember to cut out your base print first, and to work from the back of the picture to the front. The cut-out shapes I have used are shown at the top of the next page.

4. These are the cut-out pieces ready for assembly. Use the technique described on page 154 to cut round the mouse's fur. When you cut out the head, take out the middle of the left-hand ear.

5. Gently shape the dress of one of the complete images by resting it on a foam pad and rolling backwards and forwards over it with a shaping tool.

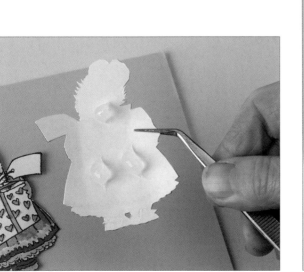

6. Apply three spots of silicone sealant to the back of the image, and a small spot to each foot.

7. Position the mouse on the base print by holding down its feet and lowering the top half into place. The mouse will then look as if it is standing on the floor and not levitating!

8. Gently shape the pantalettes, the lower half of the mouse's dress, the hem and the collar. Shape only the edges of the dress, not the middle part. Attach each piece to the base print. Tilt the dress towards the head of the mouse as you apply it so that the lower part stands out.

9. Shape the parcel. Rest it on an eraser and score down each edge of the parcel using the pointed shaping tool.

10. Using the flattened end of the shaping tool, bend the sides of the parcel back slightly to give it a three-dimensional shape.

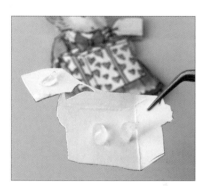

11. Hold the parcel over the base and check that it has not been folded in too far. Add two spots of silicone sealant to the back of the parcel, and one small spot to the label.

12. Attach the parcel to the base, then shape and apply the remaining pieces.

13. Cut out a 60mm (2½in) square of pink card to fit behind the aperture in the card blank.

14. Attach the piece of pink card to the inside of the aperture card using repositionable adhesive dots or double-sided tape. Fold the inside flap over the back of the pink card and glue it in place. Attach the mouse to the front of the card using double-sided tape, and add the red heart craft stickers to the four corners of the aperture.

A Gift for You

The finished card shows beautifully how watercolours can be used to create truly individual designs. The darker pink in the mouse's pantalettes and the hem of her dress is highlighted by the pink backing card and the shiny heart-shaped craft stickers. The careful shaping of the parcel accentuates the three-dimensional element of the design and gives the impression that the mouse is lifting the parcel out of the card towards the recipient.

Reflections

By using glossy silver card as a background and colouring in both sides of the two children, a reflection is created that adds an interesting dimension to this very pretty card. The silver holographic hearts enhance the effect, and make it an ideal card for a loved one.

These three cards show how versatile three-dimensional cards can be, and how backing papers and cards can be used to enhance an image.

The strong colours in the top left-hand card are brought to life by mounting the tulips on a light backing of cream card and pale green vellum.

The frog is dancing on a background created by applying yellow ink using a sponge over daisy-shaped outline craft stickers. The daisies are then removed to reveal the white outlines underneath.

Glitter Cards

by Polly Pinder

What can be more magical on a greetings card than some sparkle and glitter and little twinkling areas of colour? Just gorgeous, I love it.

There are some wonderful products available now which enable us to add this enchanting quality to our cards: glittery glues, amazing holographic papers, glinting jewels and lovely, soft, tinsel-like threads. All of these materials have different qualities: they glimmer and glisten, they are bright and shiny, they glow or flash or shimmer. What could be nicer? And in the spirit of the recycling philosophy which now abounds (and which we card makers have been aware of for years), many of the cards in this book have utilised any glittery things which would otherwise have been discarded – used Christmas cards, gift wrap, Christmas crackers, carrier bags, chocolate wrapping and anything I could gather without looking too conspicuously odd! My family are now used to a kind of hovering behaviour; a surreptitious glance at their wastepaper baskets; questioning looks which mean 'You're not throwing that away are you?'. I have even been known to retrieve suitable items from the dustbin, while the family looked on in quiet horror. Never mind; no-one is aware that the cards they so happily receive have very interesting histories.

I hope you will be inspired to follow some of the ideas in this section and perhaps go on to develop your own. Making cards for family and friends is one of the most pleasurable occupations, and long may it remain so.

Polly

Simple designs made special by bits of sparkle. Rubber stamps, old greetings cards, metallic confetti and a used carrier bag have all helped to produce this varied collection of cards.

Materials

Card and papers

In addition to the wonderful textured and patterned papers which we have become accustomed to using for our handmade cards, there are now spectacular holographic papers available. These, along with brilliantly coloured foils, make the job of card creation even more exciting. They can be used as a backdrop in contrast to matt papers, or as tiny cut-outs to add glints of sparkle. They can become shimmering borders for an otherwise subdued design or surprising inserts and inlays. They really are fascinating and the printing process and inks which create these complex images are a great wonder to me.

Sparkly card can be bought, and it is also possible to make your own using tubes of glitter, fine or coarse, liberally sprinkled on to a thin layer of PVA glue.

Some of the many stunning papers and cards which can be used to add lustre to your card designs.

Glittery embellishments

Although many of these items have been around for some time, especially those associated with stamping, there are now even more available – things as diverse as sparkly pipe cleaners and shiny metal confetti; soft, tinsel-like thread, glinting net and wonderful glues positively bursting with vibrantly coloured glitter. Outline stickers are a product which can fire the imagination. They can be very intricate so the card design which includes them should be relatively uncluttered. Contrasts are always good – shiny and matt, bright and subdued, complex and simple.

All of these items can be bought at craft stores, and they prove inexpensive when you consider how little is required for each card.

Stamp and embossing materials

The embossing area of stamping and the vast array of beautifully intricate stamps have given a professional look to our cards and another opportunity to discover imaginative ways of designing and presenting them. The stamps, inkpads, embossing pens and powders, and heat gun are essential for the production of the Fabulous Fairy Dust card.

Shiny embossing powders have given a new dimension to the concept of stamping.

Tip
Care needs to be taken with the heat gun; the tip can get very hot indeed.

Other items

Cutting tools: Ordinary sharp scissors are essential and, if you have them, cuticle scissors are very useful for cutting out circles and other curved shapes. Circle aperture cutters are an excellent way of achieving a perfectly smooth, round opening. A good quality steel-handled craft knife is best, with some spare blades – it is possible to sharpen these on an oil stone. The knife should be used in conjunction with a self-healing cutting mat and a steel ruler. The little craft punches of heart, flower and star designs are very useful for either punching out or sticking on. Fancy-edged scissors are also an important cutting tool for the card maker.

Glues: I have used water-based glue sticks, PVA glue and double-sided tape throughout the book. They are all useful for different jobs. You can also use clear all-purpose glue.

Drawing and painting materials: You will need tracing paper and a pencil to transfer the images for some of the cards. A pencil sharpener and eraser might also be useful. Watercolour paints and brushes can be used to add colour to your cards.

Crimping machine: This is used to give a corrugated look to stiff paper and card. I have used it for the card on page 185 to give the appearance of snow drifting in different directions.

A **palette knife** and an **old paintbrush** are useful for spreading PVA and glitter glues.

A **knitting needle** can be used for creasing cards if you are cutting your own.

Essential equipment used for making the cards in this section.

Basic techniques

Glitter glue

1. Put the initial drop of glue on to your card then lift the nozzle very slightly. Pipe your design, allowing the trail of glue to fall on to the surface.

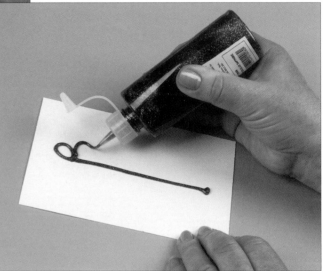

2. Continue your design. Have a little practice first – the glue can always be scraped up and put back in its container.

3. The glue can be spread on the card using an artist's palette knife to give a lovely impression of glitter dust.

Loose glitter

1. Spread a thin film of PVA glue on to your card using an artist's palette knife.

2. Sprinkle liberally with glitter.

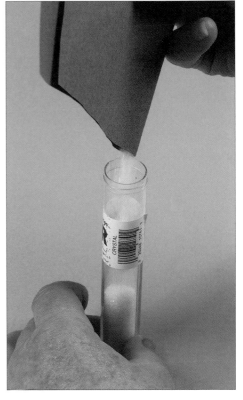

3. Tap the side of the card to shake off excess glitter.

4. Pour the excess back into the container.

Glittering Christmas Trees

You will need
Blank blue card,
100 x 210mm (4 x 8¼in)

White mulberry tissue,
100 x 210mm (4 x 8¼in)

Highly textured green paper,
70 x 130mm (3 x 5in)

Bright red card, 50 x 70mm
(2 x 3in)

Small piece of glittered
gold card

Various coloured
holographic papers

Red glitter glue

Office punch, little and
medium star punches

Tracing paper, pencil and ruler

Craft knife and cutting mat

Glue stick and
double-sided tape

This is so simple. I have used wonderful holographic self-adhesive papers for the tree decorations, all of which are cut using an ordinary office punch and small decorative punches. The indent on the planter was made with the handle of my craft knife and emphasises the rim, giving a slight 3D effect. The planter decoration was squeezed from a small glitter glue tube; this takes some time to dry so it is best to leave it until last.

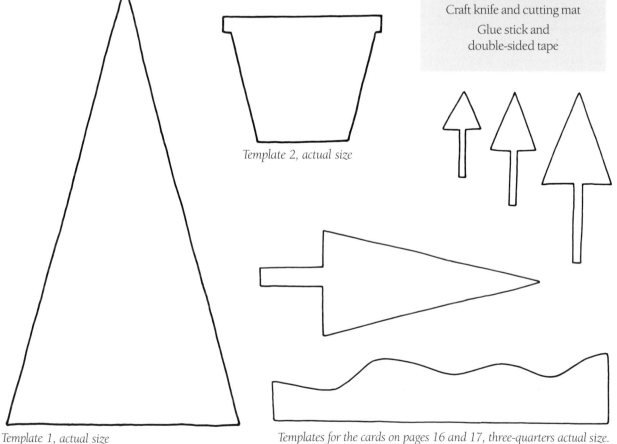

Template 2, actual size

Template 1, actual size

Templates for the cards on pages 16 and 17, three-quarters actual size.

Tip
If making your own blank
card use a thick knitting
needle to score the fold
(on the inside). The
needle is also useful for
indenting little patterns
on card.

1. Tear the edges from the mulberry tissue to roughly 80 x 185mm
(3¼ x 7¼in) then, using the glue stick, secure it to the card.

2. Trace the tree
shape opposite
(template 1) and
transfer it on to the
textured green paper.
Cut it out and, using
the double-sided
tape, secure it to the
mulberry tissue.

3. Attach double-sided tape to the back of the holographic papers and glittered gold card. Punch out the baubles (nine) and stars (eleven) and the gold star for the tree top. Remove the backing, using the point of your craft knife, and press the baubles and small stars on to the tree.

4. Trace the planter on to the red card and, just before cutting it out, lay your ruler along the top and make an indent with your knife handle (or a knitting needle) to create the lip edge.

5. Using the glitter glue, make a simple pattern just beneath the rim. When the glue has dried (a couple of hours) position the planter under the tree using double-sided tape to secure.

6. Attach the gold star to the top of the tree.

Glitter glue is lovely. One is tempted to squeeze it all over the place, but a little restraint is necessary for the sake of the finished card. Here the matt, deeply textured tree contrasts well with the twinkling decorations.

A subtly textured pearlescent paper was used as a background for this magnificent tree. I traced the tree on to a piece of dark green card, covered it with double-sided tape then cut and stuck a shimmering pipe cleaner to form the trunk. The branches were then cut and attached. The planter is matt gold card with shiny gold stars under the rim.

Right, top: These holographic trees were cut from a carrier bag. The central one is attached with 3D foam squares to give a slight depth to the image. The glittery snow and star (cut using a craft punch) were taken from one of last year's Christmas cards.

Right, bottom: For this very simple design a piece of white card was put through the crimping machine. Three sections were cut from it with the ridges going in different directions. These were attached to the blank white card using double-sided tape. The trees were cut from silver holographic paper with a self-adhesive backing.

Fabulous Fairy Dust

This project brings to mind the character of Tinkerbell from *Peter Pan* and the trail of sparkly dust she left as she flew about performing mischief.

I have used stamps for these cards because they are so pretty, beautifully detailed and lend themselves to delicate sparkling effects. To achieve the best results for the semi-transparent look on the dress and wings, you will need to use watercolour paints, watercolour paper and a brush with a fine point. The technique is to lay a flat wash, then remove some of the colour using a clean, damp brush. In order to make a colour paler you simply add water; never add white paint. Have a little practice before starting. The open-weave tissue paper is very soft and easy to tear if you hold it firmly.

You will need

Blank white card,
100 x 135mm (4 x 5¼in)

Blue sparkle card,
90 x 125mm (3½ x 5in)

White open-weave tissue,
90 x 125mm (3½ x 5in)

Watercolour paints

Watercolour paper,
90 x 125mm (3½ x 5in)

Paintbrush with a fine point

Fairy stamp

Sparkle-silver and sparkle-white embossing powders

Embossing inkpad and embossing heat gun

Tracing paper and pencil

Scissors and/or cuticle scissors

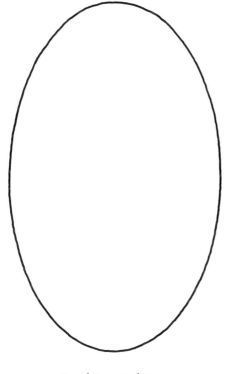

Template, actual size

1. Put pieces of double-sided tape on to the back of the blue sparkle card and position it centrally on to the blank white card.

Tip
When using the heat gun, watch carefully for the powder to melt, just a few seconds, then remove the heat gun immediately to avoid scorching the paper.

2. Press the stamp on to the embossing inkpad. Stamp it on to the centre of the watercolour paper. Sprinkle the image liberally with the silver powder.

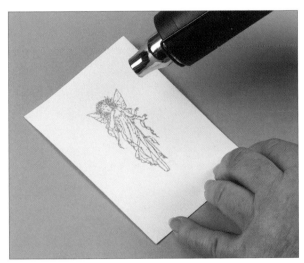

3. Have ready a sheet of spare paper, then tap the watercolour paper on its side to remove the excess powder. Pour the powder back into its container. Use the heat gun to melt the powder.

4. Paint the fairy, removing some areas of colour with a clean, damp brush to give a semi-transparent effect. I used French ultramarine for the dress, cerulean blue for the wings and very watery alizarin crimson with a touch of cadmium yellow for the skin tone.

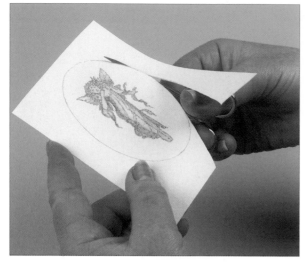

5. Transfer the oval to the watercolour paper, then carefully cut it out, using a pair of cuticle scissors if you have some.

6. Holding the oval, gently press the edge, all the way round, on to the embossing pad. Sprinkle liberally with the white powder then use the heat gun to melt it, just as before.

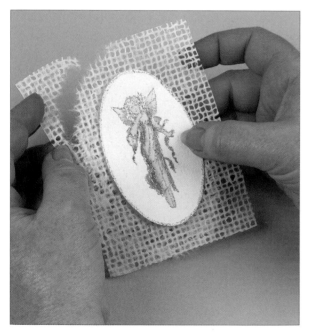

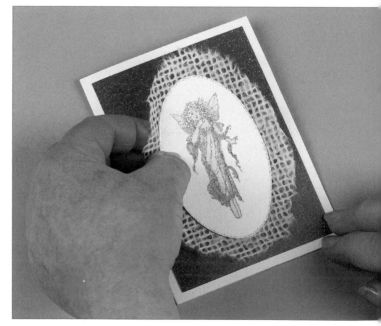

7. Put a piece of double-sided tape on to the back of the oval, then attach it to the centre of the open-weave tissue paper. Carefully tear the tissue following the curve of the oval.

8. Attach the oval and tissue paper to the card using double-sided tape.

An oval seemed to be the perfect shape to frame this little fairy, backed by an open-weave tissue paper to soften the shape.

This fairy stamp is quite complex – the added lavender, leaves and butterfly mean that the design of the card should be very simple. When painting the fairy I tried to replicate the soft rainbow colours of the foil paper (originally gift wrap). Notice how some of the paint has been removed from the dress and wings to give a feeling of lightness.

Top: *This reminds me of those charming Parisian net hats of the fifties, simple and alluring. A square of purple card was covered with glitter net. Another length was gathered, tied with silver thread and attached to the card with double-sided tape. The oval was positioned and the sides of the net tucked into the sides of the square.*

Bottom: *It is very difficult to emboss successfully on mulberry tissue. Here I have used ordinary tissue, in the same delicate pink, and stuck it on top of the torn mulberry tissue using just a sliver of double-sided tape. It is even possible to paint on the ordinary tissue without causing it to cockle. The little glittery flowers were punched from an old birthday card.*

Index